the directory of FLAGS

the directory of FLAGS

A GUIDE TO FLAGS FROM AROUND THE WORLD   *Charlotte Greig*

Ivy Press

This edition published in 2015 by
Ivy Press
An imprint of The Quarto Group
The Old Brewery, 6 Blundell Street
London N7 9BH, United Kingdom
T (0)20 7700 6700 **F** (0)20 7700 8066
www.QuartoKnows.com

First published in 2005

British Library Cataloguing-in-Publication Data
A catalogue record for this book is available from the British Library

ISBN: 978-1-78240-281-7

This book was conceived, designed and produced by
Ivy Press
58 West Street, Brighton BN1 2RA, UK

Creative Director Michael Whitehead
Publisher Susan Kelly
Editorial Director Jason Hook
Senior Project Editor Rebecca Saraceno
Editorial Assistant Andrew Peters
Designer Tony Seddon

Printed in China

10 9 8 7 6 5 4 3 2

MIX
Paper from
responsible sources
FSC® C104723

Contents

Introduction

Flags have been used all over the world for thousands of years to identify peoples, places, cultures, and beliefs. From earliest times, cloth banners were used in the East. However, in the West, the first flaglike objects were vexilloids, carved staffs used to protect and bring

Commonwealth of Nations

victory to the bearer. The soldiers of ancient Rome, for example, carried standards ornamented with eagles. Later, in the twelfth and thirteenth centuries, the Christian crusaders introduced banners to identify their armies in battle. In particular, they used the

Soloman Islands

Christian cross, which today appears on European flags in various guises (as the St. George cross, the saltire, the Greek cross, the off-center Scandinavian cross, and so on).

Islam also has a long history of flags, dating back to its earliest founding dynasties: red

Moldova

for the Khawarij; white for the Umayyad; black for the Abbasid; and green for the Fatimid. Later, just as the cross had been used to rally Christendom,

the crescent was displayed to unite the Muslim world. Today, the symbol of the crescent, and the ancient dynastic colors of Islam, still dominate the flags of the Arab nations.

In medieval Europe, banners, pennants, and coats of arms were used to identify monarchs, families, cities, and regions. Many of these heraldic designs still appear on European flags. But it was not until the seventeenth century that official national flags began to emerge. Some were the result of political unions, such as the Union Flag (also called the Union Jack) of Great Britain, adopted in 1606. But many had their origins in banners of political groups fighting for nationalist causes. The most famous of these is the tricolor, which became a powerful symbol of freedom during the French Revolution of 1789, and since then has influenced the design of countless national flags across the globe. From the eighteenth century onward, many countries in all continents fought to free themselves from

centuries of colonial rule by the Western European nations. In the nineteenth century, newborn South American republics celebrated their new-found freedom with flags that reflected both their past struggles and their optimism for the future. In the twentieth century, many former British colonies achieved independence; some retained the Union Jack on their flags and others created vibrant new designs based on their indigenous cultures.

Kazakhstan

Today, the flags of the world provide a fascinating document of each country's national identity: from past struggles to current political alliances; beliefs, whether religious or secular; even art and culture. The flags in this book are organized geographically, rather than alphabetically, or in terms of political borders. Thus, the Turkish flag will be found in the section on Asia rather than Europe, within a group that includes its nearby neighbors: Cyprus, Armenia, and Syria. In this way, important historical, cultural, and ideological links between countries, as symbolized on their flags, can be seen more clearly. For example,

Niue

in Eastern Europe, we find that flag designs are often based around the colors red, blue, and white, which date back to the pre-Communist Russian tricolor, revived again after the collapse of the USSR. In Arabic countries, the design of a white or red crescent moon and stars on a green background is prevalent, making reference to Islamic religious beliefs in this part of the world. And in Africa, during the 1960s when many new flags were established as countries became independent, various designs featuring the colors red, yellow, and green, remind us of Africa's history of resistance to colonialism.

Jamaica

The book gives factual information on each flag, such as the date it was adopted and its proportions (the ratio 1:2 means height 1 to length 2) and general information about the countries or states listed, such as the main languages spoken (but often for reasons of space it was impossible to include every one). The facts are taken from a variety of reliable sources, in particular the regularly updated CIA World Factbook (see page 206).

THE AMERICAS

The Americas have a wealth of national flags that reflect both their history of colonization by Europe and their struggle for independence. The U.S. flag is a case in point. Its red, white, and blue colors reflect its links with Britain, while its design of stars and stripes symbolizes its status as a sovereign nation. In the same way, the colors of the Canadian flag refer to the English cross of St. George, while the maple leaf represents Canada's indigenous people. In the Caribbean, some islands have retained the Union Jack on their flags, while others have adopted entirely new designs. This tension between past and present is again apparent in the flags of the South American republics: on the one hand, rifles and bayonets symbolize their history of struggle against Spanish colonialism, and on the other, rainbows and sunrises show their optimism for the future.

United States of America

Capital city *Washington DC*
Population *318,892,103*
Land area (sq. mi) *3,794,083;* **(sq. km)** *9,826,675*
Currency *1 U.S. dollar = 100 cents*
Main languages *English, Spanish*
Ratio 10:19

The United States flag first came into being in 1777. It was almost certainly designed by Congressman Francis Hopkinson and based on the flag of the Sons of Liberty, a group of activists who had rebelled against British taxation in the American colonies. The 13 red stripes on a white background represented the first colonies to band together in opposition to British rule. Originally, there were also 13 stars on the flag, formed into a circle. As more states joined the union, more stars and stripes were added, until there was no room left. Various designs evolved, but it was not until 1912 that a standard flag was approved, with 13 stripes, designating the original states, and the stars of the new member states in rows. During the nineteenth and twentieth centuries, the number of stars grew from 13 to 50.

Canada

Capital city *Ottawa*
Population *34,834,841*
Land area (sq. mi) *3,855,085;* **(sq. km)** *9,984,670*
Currency *1 Canadian dollar = 100 cents*
Main languages *English, French, Inuktitut*
Ratio 1:2

On February 15, 1965, the newly created national flag of Canada was flown for the first time on Parliament Hill, Ottawa, in the presence of Prime Minister Lester B. Pearson and thousands of Canadian citizens. Designed by Dr. George Stanley, it featured a stylized red maple leaf on a white background, with two red stripes either side. The design incorporates many elements of Canadian history. The maple leaf symbolizes Canada's indigenous people, who for centuries have used maple sap as a source of food. Later, in the twentieth century, the symbol of the maple leaf was adopted by Canadian athletes, and by Canadian soldiers in World Wars I and II. The red and white colors make reference to Canada's links with Britain, in particular to the St. George's Cross flag.

Saint Pierre and Miquelon

Capital city *Saint-Pierre*
Population *6,995*
Land area (sq. mi) *93;* **(sq. km)** *242*
Currency *1 euro = 100 cents*
Languages *French, English*

Ratio 2:3

The islands of Saint Pierre and Miquelon were first settled by the French in the early seventeenth century. Today, these small islands in the North Atlantic are all that remain of France's once vast territories in the area. To symbolize their history of settlement, the islands' local flag shows a large yellow sailing ship against a blue background, which is bordered by three designs on the hoist side. The top one shows the Ikurrina flag of the Basque country; the black and white pattern in the middle represents Brittany, and the two yellow lions on a red background at the bottom represent Normandy.

Puerto Rico

Capital city *San Juan*
Population *3,897,960*
Land area (sq. mi) *5324;* **(sq. km)** *13,790*
Currency *1 U.S. dollar = 100 cents*
Languages *Spanish, English*

Ratio 2:3

The Caribbean island of Puerto Rico was ruled for centuries from 1493 by the Spanish, who brought many African slaves into the country and almost destroyed the indigenous population. In 1898, after the Spanish-American war, Puerto Rico was ceded to the U.S., and its people were granted U.S. citizenship in 1917. The design of the island's flag reflects these links with the U.S.: bold red and white stripes and a single white star on a blue background recall the Stars and Stripes. The flag is similar to that of Cuba, except that the colors of the stripes and triangle are reversed.

Virgin Islands

Capital city *Charlotte Amalie*
Population *108,775*
Land area (sq. mi) *136;* **(sq. km)** *1910*
Currency *1 U.S. dollar = 100 cents*
Languages *English, Spanish, Creole*

Ratio 2:3

During the seventeenth century, the archipelago known as the Virgin Islands was divided between the English and the Danish, who imported slave labor from Africa to produce sugar cane there. In 1917, the U.S. bought the Danish section of the territory, which today is a top vacation destination for American tourists. The flag of the U.S. Virgin Islands, adopted in 1921, shows the letters VI in azure blue, and between them an American eagle with the U.S. shield on its breast, holding a sprig of laurel in one talon and three arrows (representing the three main islands) in the other.

British Virgin Islands

Capital city *Road Town*
Population *32,680*
Land area (sq. mi) *58;* **(sq. km)** *151*
Currency *1 U.S. dollar = 100 cents*
Languages *English, Spanish*

Ratio 1:2

Christopher Columbus is believed to have named these islands "Las Virgenes" after St. Ursula, who according to Christian myth was martyred together with eleven thousand virgin companions. The islands were annexed by the English in 1672, although today the prosperous tourist economy is more closely linked to the larger and more populous U.S. Virgin Islands. The present flag, showing the figure of St. Ursula with the inscription "Vigilate" ("Be Watchful"), was adopted in 1956. Each of the eleven lamps surrounding the saint represents a thousand virgins.

Cuba

Capital city *Havana*

Population *11,308,764*

Land area (sq. mi) *42,803;* **(sq. km)** *110,860*

Currency *1 Cuban peso = 100 centavos*

Language *Spanish, English*

Ratio 1:2

The Cuban flag was designed by Narciso Lopez in 1849, and adopted as the national flag on May 20, 1902. Lopez was a military adventurer of Venezuelan origin, who tried to help Cuba break away from Spanish rule and incorporate it into the United States. The single star on his flag, known as the "Estrella Solitaria" or Lone Star, was initially designed to one day take its place on the U.S. flag, the Stars and Stripes. Lopez's attempt failed, and instead, Cuba became a Communist state. Today, the official explanation for the flag is that the three blue stripes represent the three former provinces of the island. The red triangle represents the blood shed by revolutionaries in the pursuit of freedom and the single star is a symbol of unity.

Antigua and Barbuda

Capital city *Saint John's (Antigua)*
Population *91,295*
Land area (sq. mi) *170;* **(sq. km)** *441*
Currency *1 East Caribbean dollar = 100 cents*
Languages *English, local dialects*

Ratio 2:3

The national flag of Antigua and Barbuda was designed by Reginald Samuels, an art teacher in an Antiguan high school. Adopted in 1967, the year that the islands became self-governing, the design of the flag makes reference both to their history and to their people's hopes for the future. The rising sun represents the dawning of a new era, while the red triangles symbolize the energy of the people. Blue stands for hope, and black for the islanders' African ancestry. The color combination of yellow, blue, and white is intended to represent the islands' landscape of sun, sand, and sea.

The Bahamas

Capital city *Nassau*
Population *321,834*
Land area (sq. mi) *5,359;* **(sq. km)** *13,880*
Currency *1 Bahamian dollar = 100 cents*
Languages *English, Creole*

Ratio 1:2

The islands of the Bahamas were first settled by the British in 1647, and then became a British colony in 1783. They were governed by the British until 1973, when they gained independence. Since then, the Bahamas has become a wealthy center for tourism and commerce, as well as an illegal shipment point for the trafficking of drugs and migrant workers into the U.S. The Bahamian flag, with its colors of aquamarine and gold, is said to represent the ocean waters around the golden sands surrounding the islands, while the black triangle denotes the African heritage of the islands' people.

Barbados

Capital city *Bridgetown*
Population *289,680*
Land area (sq. mi) *166;* **(sq. km)** *430*
Currency *1 Barbadian dollar = 100 cents*
Language *English, Bajan*

Ratio 2:3

The British settled Barbados in the seventeenth century and established sugar plantations there, using slave labor from Africa. After the abolition of slavery in 1834, the island's economy continued to be dominated by sugar production, until a series of reforms took place in the twentieth century. In 1966, Barbados achieved independence from Britain. To mark this break with its colonial past, the Barbadian flag shows a trident broken off at the head (originally, the island's coat of arms showed the complete trident of Britannia). The three vertical bands of blue, gold, and blue represent sky, sand, and sea respectively.

Cayman Islands

Capital city *George Town*
Population *54,914*
Land area (sq. mi) *101;* **(sq. km)** *264*
Currency *1 Caymanian dollar = 100 cents*
Language *English*

Ratio 1:2

During the eighteenth century, the British ruled Jamaica and began their colonization of the nearby Cayman Islands. After Jamaica achieved independence in 1962, the islands remained under British rule, becoming a center for offshore banking and prestige tourism. Their status today as a British Overseas Territory is reflected in their flag. On the hoist side is the Union Jack, while on the right is the Caymanian coat of arms, showing a turtle and a pineapple over a shield. The three stars on the shield denote the three islands, while underneath is the motto: "He hath founded it upon the seas."

Dominica

Capital city *Roseau*
Population *73,449*
Land area (sq. mi) *291;* **(sq. km)** *751*
Currency *1 East Caribbean dollar = 100 cents*
Languages *English, French patois*

Ratio 1:2

The national flag of Dominica, adopted in 1978, reflects many facets of the island's history and its current importance as one of the most ecologically varied areas of the Caribbean. In the center of the flag is the Sisserou Parrot, Dominica's National Bird, surrounded by ten green stars, denoting the island's ten parishes. The yellow stripe represents the island's original inhabitants, the Caribs, and its main crops of bananas and citrus. The black stripe symbolizes the African heritage of the island's people, and its rich volcanic soil, while the white one is intended to reflect its clear rivers and waterfalls.

Grenada

Capital city *Saint George's*
Population *110,152*
Land area (sq. mi) *133;* **(sq. km)** *344*
Currency *1 East Caribbean dollar = 100 cents*
Languages *English, French patois*

Ratio 3:5

Grenada's national flag, with its vibrant colors of yellow, red, and green reflects the warmth and vitality of its people rather than its turbulent history. (It achieved independence from colonial rule in 1974, and was later invaded by the U.S., which overthrew the Marxist government there.) The central yellow star on the flag stands for the borough of the capital Saint George's, while the six stars on its red border denote the other parishes of the islands. To the left of the central star is a symbol representing a nutmeg, one of the major export crops of the island.

Haiti

Capital city *Port-au-Prince*
Population *9,996,731*
Land area (sq. mi) *10,714;* **(sq. km)** *27,750*
Currency *1 gourde = 100 centimes*
Languages *French, Creole*

Ratio 3:5

Haiti is the western third of the Caribbean island of Hispaniola; the other two-thirds make up the Dominican Republic. Today, after a long history of colonial exploitation and political turmoil, Haiti has emerged as the poorest country in the western hemisphere. However, Haiti also has an inspiring history of resistance. In 1804, after a massive slave uprising led by Toussaint L'Ouverture, it declared itself the first independent Black republic. The country's flag, adopted in 1986, reflects its pride in this history. On a red and blue ground, within a white rectangle, the flag shows the coat of arms of the republic with a palm, cannons, and the liberty cap (a cap worn in ancient times by freed slaves). The motto underneath reads "L'Union Fait La Force" ("Strength in Unity").

Dominican Republic

Capital city *Santo Domingo*
Population *10,349,741*
Land area (sq. mi) *18,791;* **(sq. km)** *48,670*
Currency *1 Dominican peso = 100 centavos*
Language *Spanish*

Ratio 5:8

The Dominican Republic comprises two-thirds of the island of Hispaniola. Claimed by Columbus in the fifteenth century, the island remained in Spanish hands until 1804, when the French claimed the western third of the island as Haiti. The remaining two-thirds became known as Santo Domingo until 1844, when it achieved independence and became the Dominican Republic. Today, its flag shows the republic's coat of arms, a shield supported by an olive branch on one side and a palm branch on the other, with the inscription, "Dios, Patria, Libertad" ("God, Country, Freedom").

Trinidad and Tobago

Capital city *Port-of-Spain*
Population *1,223,916*
Land area (sq. mi) *1,980;* **(sq. km)** *5,128*
Currency *1 Trinidad & Tobago dollar = 100 cents*
Main languages *English, Hindi, French*

Ratio 3:5

The islands of Trinidad and Tobago gained their independence in 1962, after centuries of colonial rule. The Spanish, Dutch, French, and British all fought over them, eventually ceding them to the British, who brought in workers from India to replace African slave labor on the plantations. As a result of this legacy, the islands now have one of the most multicultural populations in the world. Accordingly, the national flag has been designed to emphasize unity. It consists of a red ground with a single black band, edged in white, running from the upper hoist side to the lower fly side.

Jamaica

Capital city *Kingston*

Population *2,930,050*

Land area (sq. mi) *4,244;* **(sq. km)** *10,991*

Currency *1 Jamaican dollar = 100 cents*

Languages *English, English patois*

Ratio 1:2

The Jamaican flag was adopted in 1962, when the island gained full independence within the British Commonwealth. For centuries, it had been part of the British Empire, becoming one of the largest slave-trading centers in the world. When slavery was abolished there in 1838, the island underwent violent upheaval, which successive governments failed to quell. Today, poor economic conditions and high levels of crime continue to beset Jamaica, so that the island still struggles to maintain social and economic stability. The design of the nation's flag reflects this turbulent history; it is said to illustrate the motto: "Hardships there are but the land is green and the sun shineth." It shows a gold saltire (or diagonal cross) against two black triangles at the sides and two green ones above and below.

St. Kitts and Nevis

Capital city *Basseterre*
Population *51,538*
Land area (sq. mi) *100;* **(sq. km)** *261*
Currency *1 East Caribbean dollar = 100 cents*
Language *English*

Ratio 2:3

The two white, five-pointed stars on the national flag of St. Kitts-Nevis are commonly thought to represent these two leeward islands of the Caribbean. However, this is not so: the two stars actually stand for hope and liberty. St. Kitts was first named by Christopher Columbus in 1493, and was fought over by the British and the French, until 1783 when it was ceded to Britain. In 1871, St. Kitts-Nevis, together with nearby Anguilla, united to form a British dependency, but later Anguilla withdrew. In 1983, St. Kitts-Nevis became fully independent within the British Commonwealth.

St. Lucia

Capital city *Castries*
Population *164,213*
Land area (sq. mi) *238;* **(sq. km)** *616*
Currency *1 East Caribbean dollar = 100 cents*
Languages *English, French patois*

Ratio 1:2

The national flag of St. Lucia was adopted in 1979, when the island achieved independence from British colonial rule. Its design shows a gold and black triangle, bordered in white, set in a blue ground. Designed by local artist Dunstan St. Omer, the flag represents the island surrounded by the sea. The two triangular shapes represent the Pitons, a distinctive pair of volcanic rocks on the island which are recognized, both locally and worldwide, as symbols of St. Lucia. In recent years, the color of the flag's background, representing the sea, has changed from a dark to a lighter blue.

St. Vincent and the Grenadines

Capital city *Kingstown*
Population *117,193*
Land area (sq. mi) *150;* **(sq. km)** *389*
Currency *1 East Caribbean dollar = 100 cents*
Languages *English, French patois*

Ratio 2:3

During the eighteenth century, the French and the British fought over these islands, until in 1783, they were ceded to Britain. In 1979, St. Vincent and the Grenadines achieved independence. The design of the current national flag, adopted in 1985, reflects the islands' status in history as "gems of the Antilles," with a pattern of green diamonds in a "V" shape, representing the many islands (over 600) in the group. The blue, gold, and green vertical bands are intended to refer to the islands' beautiful landscape of sky, sand, and lush vegetation. The flag is sometimes known as "the gems."

Anguilla

Capital city *The Valley*
Population *16,086*
Land area (sq. mi) *35;* **(sq. km)** *91*
Currency *1 East Caribbean dollar = 100 cents*
Language *English*

Ratio 1:2

The flag of Anguilla shows a blue ensign with the Union Jack on the upper hoist side, and on the outer side, the Anguillan coat of arms, with three dolphins in a circular pattern symbolizing friendship, wisdom, and strength. In this way, the design refers both to Anguilla's close links with Britain, and to its independent stance. Settled in 1650 by the British, the island later became a single British dependency along with neighboring St. Kitts-Nevis. The islanders never accepted this situation, and agitated to become a separate British dependency, a status that was formally granted in 1980.

Bermuda

Capital city *Hamilton*
Population *69,839*
Land area (sq. mi) *20*; **(sq. km)** *54*
Currency *1 Bermudan dollar = 100 cents*
Languages *English, Portuguese*

Ratio 1:2

Bermuda was discovered by a Spanish explorer, Juan de Bermudez, in 1503, but was not settled by Europeans until over a century later, when an English ship, the Sea Venture, was wrecked there during a hurricane. Its crew were traveling to the Jamestown settlement in Virginia, but instead stayed on the island to establish a new colony. Today, Bermuda's national flag records this event. On the upper hoist side is the Union Flag, while on the lower fly side is the Bermudan coat of arms—a shield, held by a red lion, showing the wreck of the Sea Venture.

Montserrat

Capital city *Plymouth*
Population *9,245*
Land area (sq. mi) *39*; **(sq. km)** *102*
Currency *1 East Caribbean dollar = 100 cents*
Language *English*

Ratio 1:2

Named by Christopher Columbus after a Spanish abbey on the top of a mountain, Montserrat was later settled by the British, after much fighting between various European powers. During this time, the island became known as a safe haven for Catholics; in the seventeenth century, the British ruler Oliver Cromwell sent large numbers of Irish prisoners there. The national flag of Montserrat features a British flag on the upper hoist side, and on the fly side the island's coat of arms, showing Erin, symbol of freedom in Irish legend, with her arm around a cross, holding a golden harp.

Curaçao

Capital city *Willemstad*
Population *146,839*
Land area (sq. mi) *Text;* **(sq. km)** *444*
Currency *Netherlands Antillean guilder*
Main languages *Papiamentu, Dutch*

Ratio 2:3

 The flag of Curaçao was adopted in 1984. It was the triumphant entry in a competition to which more than 2,000 designs were submitted (though some alterations were made to the winning idea). The flag's blue field is divided by a yellow horizontal stripe. The blue sections represent the Caribbean sky and sea, the yellow band the sun. The two unequally sized stars stand for the two islands that make up the country, Curaçao itself and Klein Curaçao. The five points of the stars represent the five continents—because the population of Curaçao came from every corner of the world.

Sint Maarten

Capital city *Philipsburg*
Population *31,530*
Land area (sq. mi) *Text;* **(sq. km)** *34*
Currency *Netherlands Antillean guilder*
Main languages *French, English, Dutch*

Ratio 2:3

 Since 1648, the island of St. Martin has been divided between France and the Netherlands. The Dutch part of the island, known as Sint Maarten, adopted its present flag in June 1985. It consists of a horizontal bicolor, red over blue, with a white triangle at the hoist (these same colors, arranged as a tricolor, make up the national flag of the Netherlands). The coat of arms of Sint Maarten sits within the white triangle. The shield depicts Sint Maarten's courthouse along with a sprig of wild sage (the national flower) and a pelican (the national bird). The Latin motto means "Always progressing."

Costa Rica

Capital city *San José*

Population *4,755,234*

Land area (sq. mi) *19,730;* **(sq. km)** *51,100*

Currency *1 Costa Rican colon = 100 centimos*

Languages *Spanish, English*

Ratio 3:5

The flag of Costa Rica has five horizontal bands of red, white, and blue; the central red band is double the width of the others, and shows the country's coat of arms. This was first created in 1848, and redesigned in 1906, when its warlike images of cannons and rifles were taken off so as to emphasize Costa Rica's ambitions for peace. The coat of arms now shows two volcanoes, symbolizing the mountain ranges of the country, and two seas, representing the Atlantic and the Pacific. Two ships stand for its trading economy, and a rising sun signifies prosperity. Seven stars, two of which were added in 1964, stand for the country's seven provinces. It is argued that originally, the stars stood for the other central American countries.

Turks and Caicos Islands

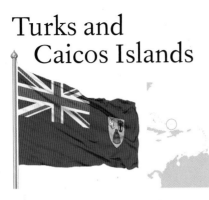

Capital city *Grand Turk (Cockburn Town)*
Population *49,070*
Land area (sq. mi) *366;* **(sq. km)** *948*
Currency *1 U.S. dollar = 100 cents*
Language *English*

Ratio 1:2

 As their national flag suggests, the Turks and Caicos Islands are a haven for wildlife. On the fly side, the flag features a yellow shield bearing the images of a conch, a crustacean, and a cactus. The shell is a queen conch, a type of marine snail eaten by the islanders. The crustacean is a spiny lobster, another important local food source. The cactus is a species that grows on the islands, called a Turk's head because the red fruit at the top of it resembles a fez. On the upper hoist side of the flag is the Union Jack.

El Salvador

Capital city *San Salvador*
Population *6,587,541*
Land area (sq. mi) *8,123;* **(sq. km)** *21,041*
Currency *1 U.S. dollar = 100 cents*
Languages *Spanish, Nahua*

Ratio 189:335

 The flag of El Salvador features the national coat of arms. This shows a triangle, representing the three branches of the republic (executive, legislative, and judicial), and within this five volcanoes, symbolizing the Central American isthmus. In the center is a red Phrygian cap, an ancient symbol of the freed slave. The five blue flags represent the close links between El Salvador, Guatemala, Honduras, Nicaragua, and Costa Rica; the fourteen-sectioned laurel wreath signifies the states of the republic; and the date September 15, 1821 commemorates the day El Salvador became independent.

Guatemala

Capital city *Guatemala City*

Population *14,647,083*

Land area (sq. mi) *42,042;* **(sq. km)** *108,889*

Currency *1 quetzal = 100 centavos*

Languages *Spanish, 23 Native American languages*

Ratio 5:8

The flag of Guatemala has a bold design of blue and white bands, linking it to that of the other countries of Central America, which also use these colors on their flags. Its coat of arms, in the middle of the white band, makes reference to the country's turbulent history, with a background design of crossed rifles and swords, over which is a scroll bearing the date of its independence from Spain, September 15, 1821. Perched jauntily on the scroll is the flamboyant, long-tailed quetzal, Guatemala's national bird. The whole design is framed by a wreath. Sadly, the rifles on the coat of arms continued to be emblematic of Guatemala's political situation up to the twentieth century. A long-standing guerrilla war killed and impoverished thousands of its people; it did not end until 1996.

Honduras

Capital city *Tegucigalpa*
Population *8,598,561*
Land area (sq. mi) *43,278;* **(sq. km)** *112,090*
Currency *1 lempira = 100 centavos*
Languages *Spanish, Native American dialects*

Ratio 1:2

The blue and white flag of Honduras has five white, five-pointed stars arranged in an "X" formation in the center. Both the colors of the flag and the stars symbolizes Honduras's close relationship with the other countries of Central America, which include El Salvador, Costa Rica, Nicaragua, and Guatemala. After becoming independent from Spain in 1821, these countries formed an alliance that lasted for 17 years. During the nineteenth and twentieth centuries, Honduras was ruled by a series of corrupt dictatorships, which ruined its economy, so that today it is the least developed country in Central America. Some argue that the five stars on the flag represent the hope that Honduras will once again unite with its neighboring countries in Central America.

Aruba

Capital city *Oranjestad*
Population *110,663*
Land area (sq. mi) *69;* **(sq. km)** *180*
Currency *1 Aruban florin = 100 cents*
Main languages *Papiamento, Spanish, English*
Ratio 2:3

Aruba was formerly part of the Netherlands Antilles, but seceded from the group in 1976 and today is an autonomous member of the Kingdom of the Netherlands. Its national flag, adopted at the time of independence, features a light blue ground with a red, four-pointed star on the upper hoist side and two narrow yellow bands running across the lower part. Interpretations of the yellow bands vary. They may represent gold (there was a gold rush on the island during the nineteenth century), or alternatively, a local rainflower called the wanglo that opens and lights up the landscape after rain.

Belize

Capital city *Belmopan*
Population *340,844*
Land area (sq. mi) *8,867;* **(sq. km)** *22,966*
Currency *1 Belizean dollar = 100 cents*
Main languages *Spanish, Creole, English,*
Ratio 2:3

Formerly British Honduras, Belize achieved independence in 1981, when its national flag was adopted. The flag has a blue ground with bands of red at the top and bottom, which were added to the existing flag to mark the country's independence. The rest of the flag, curiously, remained unchanged. In the center is a white disk bearing the Belizean coat of arms: two workers, one holding an ax and one an oar, stand beside a mahogany tree, with a legend underneath that reads "Sub umbra floreo" ("I flourish in the shade." This refers to Belize's history as a British colony.

Nicaragua

Capital city *Managua*

Population *5,848,641*

Land area (sq. mi) *50,335;* **(sq. km)** *130,370*

Currency *1 cordoba = 100 centavos*

Languages *Spanish, English, Native American languages*

Ratio 3:5

After centuries of colonial rule by the Spanish, Nicaragua became an independent republic in 1838, forming an alliance with its neighboring countries that lasted for several decades. Today, Nicaragua's national flag emphasizes this historic link, with the characteristic blue and white colors used by the other Central American republics. At the top and bottom of the Nicaraguan flag are wide blue bands, while a white band in the center bears the country's coat of arms. The coat of arms features five volcanoes to represent the five main Central American countries: a triangle, which stands for equality; a Phrygian cap, which is an ancient symbol of freedom; and a rainbow, which signifies peace. These symbols also appear on several other coats of arms, notably those of El Salvador and Costa Rica.

Panama

Capital city *Panama City*

Population *3,604,431*

Land area (sq. mi) *29,119;* **(sq. km)** *75,420*

Currency *1 balboa = 100 centesimos;*
1 U.S. dollar = 100 cents

Languages *Spanish, English*

Ratio 2:3

Panama's geographical position on the isthmus linking South America with Central and North America has made it a focal point for powerful trading nations throughout history. For centuries, Panama was ruled by Spain, and then by Colombia, until in 1903 it finally became independent. Immediately afterward, the U.S. began the construction of the Panama Canal, which was completed in 1914. Panama's history of continuous intrusion from abroad has created deep political conflicts within the country. Accordingly, the symbolism of its national flag expresses the desire for these to come to an end. Designed by the first president of Panama, Mr. Amador Guerrero, the flag shows two rectangles and two stars in blue and red, which stand for the political right and left, on a white ground, standing for peace.

Mexico

Capital city *Mexico City*
Population *120,286,655*
Land area (sq. mi) *758,445;* **(sq. km)** *1,964,375*
Currency *1 peso = 100 centavos*
Languages *Spanish, Native American languages*
Ratio 4:7

The dramatic flag of Mexico features three bands, one of green, one of white, and one of red. In the central white band is an eagle standing on a cactus, clutching a snake in its beak and talon. The image comes from the Mexican coat of arms, which in turn derives from an Aztec legend. The legend tells how the Aztec were guided by the god Huitzilopochtli to "seek a place where an eagle lands on a prickly pear cactus and eats a snake." They found the eagle on an island in Lake Texcoco and named it Tenochtitlan. This is now Mexico City. The colors of the flag have been variously interpreted to mean green for independence or hope, white for purity or unity, and red for union or blood.

Colombia

Colombia was first explored in 1502 by Christopher Columbus, and later became part of Spain's vast New World territories. It was not until the nineteenth century that it achieved independence from Spain. Since then, its history has been marked by violence and political instability as successive governments have struggled to control guerrilla warfare and the drug trade in the country's rural areas. In such a context, the national flag has taken on special significance as a rallying symbol for unity among the Colombian people. A popular children's song explains the yellow, blue, and red bands of the flag thus: "Yellow is our gold, blue is our vast ocean, and red is the blood that gave us our freedom." Alternative interpretations include yellow for sovereignty, blue for nobility, and red for valor.

Capital city *Bogotá*

Population *46,245,297*

Land area (sq. mi) *439,733;* **(sq. km)** *1,138,910*

Currency *1 Colombian peso = 100 centavos*

Language *Spanish*

Ratio 2:3

Suriname

Capital city *Paramaribo*
Population *573,311*
Land area (sq. mi) *63,250;* **(sq. km)** *163,820*
Currency *1 Surinamese dollar = 100 cents*
Main languages *Dutch, English, Sranang*

Ratio 2:3

Formerly Dutch Guiana, Suriname was colonized by the Dutch in 1581 and later by English traders. In 1667, the English ceded their territory to the Dutch, in exchange for New Amsterdam (now New York City). Today, as a result of its complex history of immigration and emigration, the population is a multicultural one. Accordingly, Suriname's national flag, adopted in 1975 when the country became independent from the Netherlands, shows a single star, representing the unity of all ethnic groups. The star is yellow, which stands for a golden future; the red, white, and green bands symbolize progress, peace, and hope.

Guyana

Capital city *Georgetown*
Population *735,554*
Land area (sq. mi) *83,000;* **(sq. km)** *214,970*
Currency *1 Guyanese dollar = 100 cents*
Languages *English, Native American languages*

Ratio 3:5

In 1962, the Guyanese government organized an international competition to design a national flag for the country. This was won by Whitney Smith, an American. In 1966, Guyana (formerly British Guiana) achieved independence, and Smith's design became known as "The Golden Arrowhead." The flag shows a red isosceles triangle within a yellow triangle, to form an arrowhead shape, on a green ground. The red triangle is outlined in black, the yellow in white. The red symbolizes zeal; the black, endurance; the yellow, Guyana's mineral wealth; the white, its rivers; and the green, its lush forests.

Ecuador

Capital city *Quito*

Population *15,654,411*

Land area (sq. mi) *109,482;* **(sq. km)** *283,560*

Currency *1 U.S. dollar = 100 cents*

Languages *Spanish, Quechua, Native American languages*

Ratio 2:3

In 1830, Ecuador split from Gran Colombia, a federation that also included Colombia and Venezuela. Today, Ecuador's flag echoes that of its sister countries: its bands of color, like theirs, are yellow, blue, and red. This design is attributed to General Francisco de Miranda, a Venezuelan revolutionary leader who fought against Spanish rule late in the 1700s and early 1800s. In the center of the flag is Ecuador's coat of arms, featuring a bird of prey poised to attack its enemies, with the nation under its wings. This is the Andean condor, Ecuador's national bird; weighing up to 25 pounds (11 kg) and with a wing span of 10 feet (3 m), it is the largest bird of prey in the world. In Ecuador, the national flag is often flown without the coat of arms because it difficult to reproduce.

Venezuela

Capital city *Caracas*
Population *28,868,486*
Land area (sq. mi) *352,142;* **(sq. km)** *912,050*
Currency *1 bolivar = 100 centimos*
Languages *Spanish, Native American languages and dialects*

Ratio 2:3

Venezuela's flag shares the colors of Colombia and Ecuador, with which it once formed part of Gran Colombia. These are yellow, blue and red. However, Venezuela's flag differs from the others in that its bands of color are of equal width. Yellow traditionally stood for the wealth and fertility of the country; red for the courage of the people; and blue for independence from Spain. The flag features an arc of eight white stars at its center, denoting the eight provinces of the country, which signed an Act of Independence in 1811 when Venezuela broke away from Gran Columbia. The eighth star was added in 2006, to represent the province of Guayana.

Brazil

Capital city *Brasilia*
Population *202,656,788*
Land area (sq. mi) *3,287,597*; **(sq. km)** *8,514,877*
Currency *1 real = 100 centavos*
Languages *Portuguese, Spanish, English, German*
Ratio 7:10

The Brazilian flag boasts a highly original design of a blue globe with a view of the night sky on it, as if seen from above the Earth. The position of the stars are shown as they would have been at 8.30 a.m. over Rio de Janeiro on November 15, 1889 (the date Brazil overthrew the monarchy). Each star represents a particular state; thus, for example, the state of Mato Grosso is represented by the star Sirius. The globe is set in a yellow diamond on a green background, and around it is a banner with the motto "Ordem e Progresso," meaning "Order and Progress." The idea for the flag's design came from a professor, Teixeira Mendes, who collaborated with astronomers and a painter, Decio Vilares, to create the flag.

Peru

Capital city *Lima*

Population *30,147,935*

Land area (sq. mi) *496,222;* **(sq. km)** *1,285,216*

Currency *1 nuevo sol = 100 centavos*

Languages *Spanish, Quechua, Aymara*

Ratio 2:3

The Peruvian flag consists of three wide red and white bands; in the central white band is the country's distinctive coat of arms. Designed by scientist José Gregorio Paredes and adopted in 1825, the coat of arms illustrates the animal, vegetable, and mineral wealth of the country. On the upper left-hand side is the vicuña, the national animal of Peru. A member of the camel family, the vicuña is native to the country and has never been fully domesticated. Since early times, it has been hunted for its hide and wool. On the upper right-hand side is a cinchona tree, from which quinine is made. For centuries, quinine was used to treat malaria. At the bottom of the shield is a cornucopia of coins, representing the country's rich mineral deposits.

Bolivia

Capital city *La Paz*

Population *10,631,486*

Land area (sq. mi) *424,162;* **(sq. km)** *1,098,580*

Currency *1 boliviano = 100 centavos*

Languages *Spanish, Quechua, Aymara*

Ratio 2:3

Shortly after it announced its independence from Spain in 1825, Bolivia named itself after freedom fighter Simon Bolivar. Accordingly, the republic's flag shows bands of red, green, and yellow, symbolizing the blood of Bolivia's brave revolutionary soldiers (red); the fertility of the country (green); and the country's mineral resources (yellow). In the center of the flag is the country's coat of arms. The stars on it, which have often been changed over the years, represent the country's main departments or provinces. Also shown are several distinctive elements of the Bolivian landscape, including an alpaca, a bird of prey, a breadfruit tree, and a mountain (Mount Potosí). There are also a number of weapons, such as two crossed cannon barrels, four rifles, and an Inca battle-ax, reflecting the country's turbulent history.

Paraguay

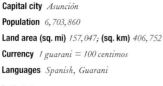

Capital city *Asunción*

Population *6,703,860*

Land area (sq. mi) *157,047;* **(sq. km)** *406,752*

Currency *1 guarani = 100 centimos*

Languages *Spanish, Guarani*

Ratio 3:5

Paraguay's national flag is unusual in that it features different designs on the front and back. On both sides, the flag has three equal horizontal bands of red, white, and blue. On the front, in the central white band is the country's national coat of arms, which consists of a yellow, five-pointed star and the legend, "República del Paraguay," surrounded by a green wreath and two circles. On the back, in the same position, is the seal of the treasury, showing a red cap of liberty (an ancient symbol of freedom) on the top of a pole, and a lion beside it, with the motto "Paz y Justicia" (Peace and Justice) displayed above. The name of the republic is also repeated on the back, and is once again surrounded by two circles.

Uruguay

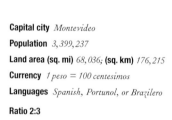

Capital city *Montevideo*

Population *3,399,237*

Land area (sq. mi) *68,036;* **(sq. km)** *176,215*

Currency *1 peso = 100 centesimos*

Languages *Spanish, Portunol, or Braᴣilero*

Ratio 2:3

 The design of Uruguay's national flag is modeled on that of the United States, with a striped main area and a contrasting section on the hoist side. The stripes of the Uruguayan flag, however, are blue and white; and to the left is the symbol of a sun. The nine stripes indicate the nine provinces that existed at the time of Uruguay's liberation from Brazilian rule in 1828. (Previously, the "Banda Oriental," or "Eastern Shore" as Uruguay was then known, had been ruled by the Spanish and then by the Portuguese from Brazil.) The sun, which is generally known as the Sun of May, has 16 rays, and bears a human face. It is a reminder of the fact that Uruguay achieved its national independence in the month of May.

Argentina

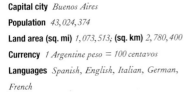

Capital city *Buenos Aires*

Population *43,024,374*

Land area (sq. mi) *1,073,513;* **(sq. km)** *2,780,400*

Currency *1 Argentine peso = 100 centavos*

Languages *Spanish, English, Italian, German, French*

Ratio 9:14

The Argentinian national flag resembles that of Uruguay in that its principal colors are light blue and white, and in addition it displays the symbol of a radiant yellow sun with a human face. The design of the flag is often attributed to General Manuel Belgrano, an Argentinian patriot of the early nineteenth century who fought against Spanish rule. Legend has it that Belgrano was inspired to choose the colors when looking at the sky just before a battle, or that he chose the colors from the cockade of his soldiers' uniforms. However, there is some debate as to whether it was actually Belgrano who designed the flag. What is clear is that the sun motif derives from images of ancient Inca gods: Inti, the Sun and Veracocha, the Creator.

Chile

Capital city *Santiago*

Population *17,363,894*

Land area (sq. mi) *291,931;* **(sq. km)** *756,102*

Currency *1 peso = 100 centavos*

Language *Spanish*

Ratio 2:3

The area we now know as Chile was once referred to as "Tchili," a Native American word meaning "snow." Today, the snow-covered Andes, which dominate the country's landscape, are represented on Chile's national flag by a white horizontal band and a white five-pointed star in the center of a blue square. The blue of the square is said to symbolize the sky. Under the white band is a longer red band, which is held to represent the blood of the people, spilled to achieve independence. The Chilean flag has obvious points of reference with the U.S. flag, not only in terms of its colors, but with its symbol of the star. The present flag came into use in the early nineteenth century, when Chile was officially proclaimed an independent nation.

Falkland Islands

Capital city *Stanley*
Population *2,967*
Land area (sq. mi) *4,700;* **(sq. km)** *12,173*
Currency *1 Falkland pound = 100 pence*
Language *English*
Ratio 1:2

The Falkland Islands, known in Spanish as Las Malvinas, have been the subject of territorial disputes for centuries. The last major dispute occurred in 1982, when the British fought an invading Argentinian force and once more laid claim to the islands. Today, the islands' flag displays the Union Jack on the upper hoist side, and the islands' coat of arms on the right, on a blue ground. The shield shows a white ram, to indicate the main activity on the islands—sheep farming—and a ship, to represent the sailing ship Desire, whose crew first discovered the islands.

South Georgia
and the South Sandwich Islands

Capital city *King Edward Point*
Population *0*
Land area (sq. mi) *1,507;* **(sq. km)** *3,903*
Currency *1 pound = 100 pence*
Language *English*
Ratio 1:2

These islands are unpopulated today, except for scientists who come to the former whaling station, Grytviken, on South Georgia, to study the local animal life. Argentina occupied the islands for a short time in 1982, but otherwise they have been administered by the British since the early twentieth century. Accordingly, the islands' flag shows the Union Jack on the upper hoist side and the national coat of arms on the right. The design on the coat of arms reflects the islands' large animal population, with a seal on the left, a penguin on the right, and a reindeer on top.

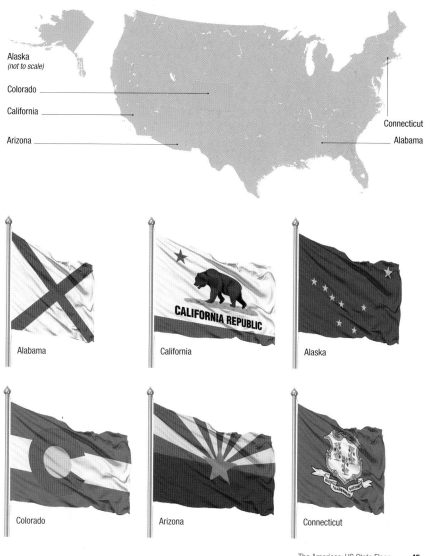

Alaska
(not to scale)

Colorado

California

Arizona

Connecticut

Alabama

Alabama

California

Alaska

Colorado

Arizona

Connecticut

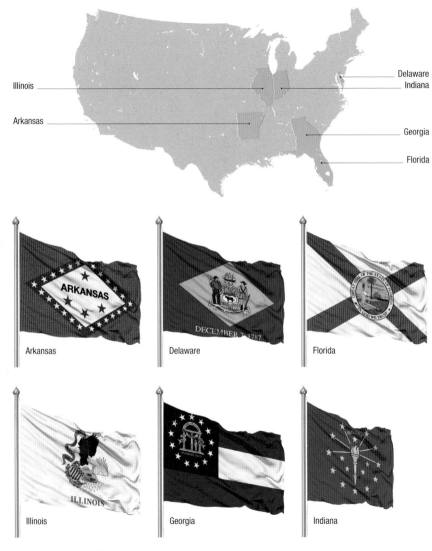

Illinois

Arkansas

Delaware
Indiana

Georgia

Florida

Arkansas

Delaware

Florida

Illinois

Georgia

Indiana

Idaho

Massachusetts

Iowa

Kansas

Kentucky

Hawaii
(not to scale)

Hawaii

Iowa

Idaho

Kansas

Kentucky

Massachusetts

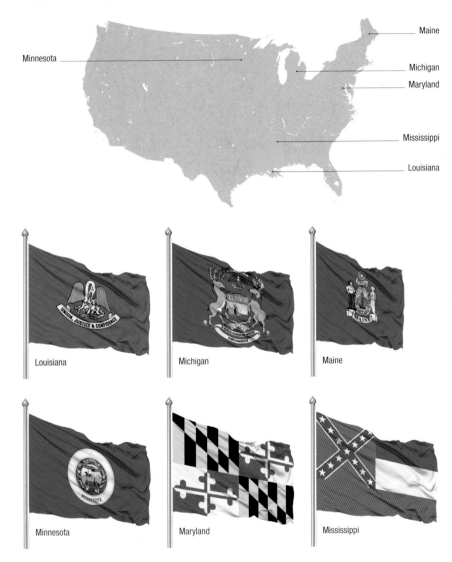

Maine

Minnesota

Michigan

Maryland

Mississippi

Louisiana

Louisiana

Michigan

Maine

Minnesota

Maryland

Mississippi

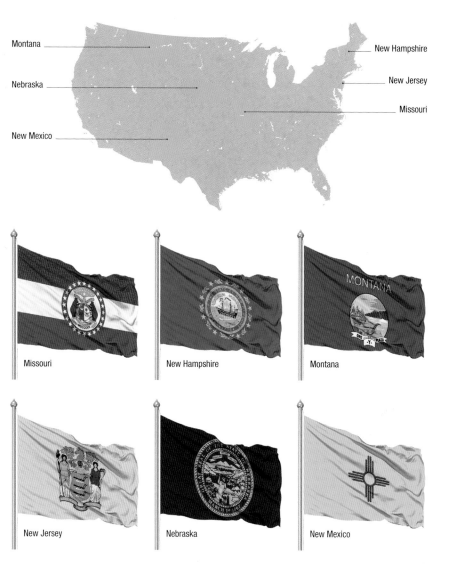

Montana

New Hampshire

Nebraska

New Jersey

Missouri

New Mexico

Missouri

New Hampshire

Montana

New Jersey

Nebraska

New Mexico

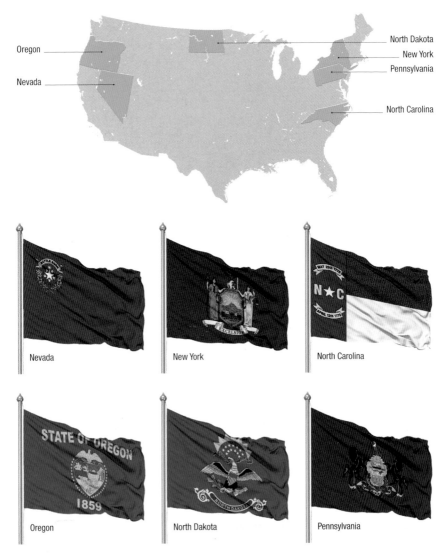

Oregon

North Dakota
New York
Pennsylvania

Nevada

North Carolina

Nevada

New York

North Carolina

Oregon

North Dakota

Pennsylvania

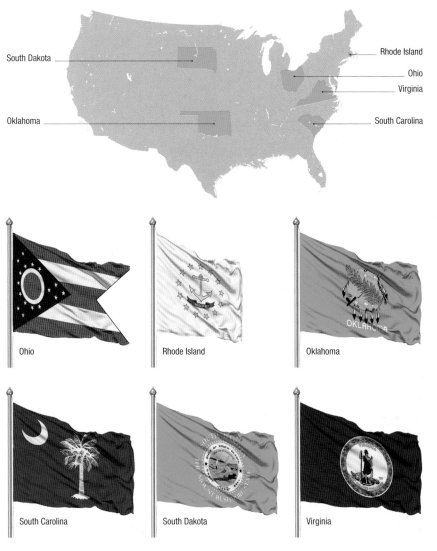

South Dakota

Rhode Island

Ohio

Virginia

Oklahoma

South Carolina

Ohio

Rhode Island

Oklahoma

South Carolina

South Dakota

Virginia

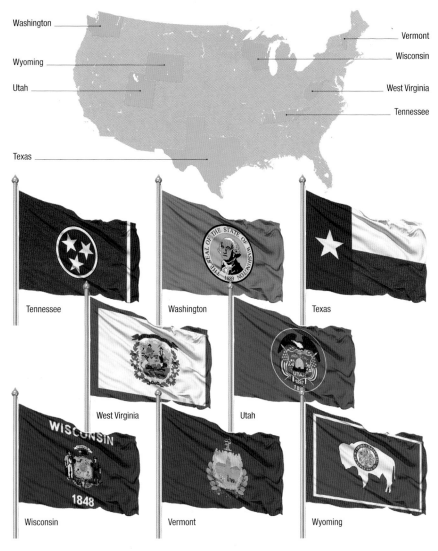

Washington

Wyoming

Utah

Texas

Vermont

Wisconsin

West Virginia

Tennessee

Tennessee

Washington

Texas

West Virginia

Utah

Wisconsin

Vermont

Wyoming

EUROPE

The heraldry of medieval times is apparent on many of the flags of Europe, especially in the use of the Christian cross. This takes many forms, such as the cross of St. George, the diagonal saltire, the couped or Greek cross, and the off-center Scandinavian cross. There are also echoes of ancient coats of arms, whether in the colors used or in the more immediately recognizable emblems that still adorn many European flags. As well as this thread of heraldry, there is also a strong element of libertarian symbolism in European flags, which is especially obvious in the use of the tricolor. The tricolor was popularized in the French revolution of 1789, but goes back to the flag of Prince William of Orange, who led a revolt in the Netherlands against Spain in the sixteenth century. In this way, both ancient and modern political ideals are represented in the flags of Europe.

Portugal

Capital city *Lisbon*

Population *10,813,834*

Land area (sq. mi) *35,555;* **(sq. km)** *92,090*

Currency *1 euro = 100 cents*

Languages *Portuguese, Mirandese*

Ratio 2:3

The Portuguese flag displays its national coat of arms on a ground of green and red; the narrower green strip symbolizing hope and the red one the blood of the Portuguese people spilled in war. The coat of arms displays a golden globe, to reflect Portugal's history as a world power during the fifteenth and sixteenth centuries, when it colonized large parts of Africa, India, and the Americas, and dominated world trade. The coat of arms also refers to Portugal's origins in the twelfth century as an independent nation: the five blue shields represent the five Moorish kings defeated by the first king of Portugal, Alfonso Henriques. The seven castles around the edge of the shield stand for the seven fortified cities that were conquered by Alfonso at that time.

Spain

Capital city *Madrid*

Population *47,737,941*

Land area (sq. mi) *195,123;* **(sq. km)** *505,370*

Currency *1 euro = 100 cents*

Languages *Castilian Spanish, Catalan, Galician, Basque*

Ratio 2:3

 The Spanish national flag has changed many times, reflecting both its internal politics and its conquests abroad (which were immense during the period of Spanish expansion in the sixteenth and seventeenth centuries). However, the colors of red and yellow have always remained the same. Today, the flag shows two horizontal bands of red at the top and bottom, with a double width of yellow in the center. On the hoist side of the central yellow band is the national coat of arms, consisting of the royal seal, and on either side of it, the pillars of Hercules. These pillars represent Gibraltar and Ceuta, which lie on either side of the Strait of Gibraltar. The Spanish flag is often flown in a simplified version, without the national coat of arms on it.

France

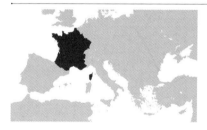

Capital city *Paris*
Population *66,259,012*
Land area (sq. mi) *248,571;* **(sq. km)** *643,801*
Currency *1 euro = 100 cents*
Languages *French, regional languages and dialects*
Ratio 2:3

The famous French tricolor displays the colors of blue on the hoist side, white in the middle, and red on the right. The three bands are of equal width. The flag was created as a symbol of freedom during the period of the French Revolution in the late eighteenth century, when the people rebelled against the tyranny of the monarchy. The colors are thought to have come from the red, white, and blue cockade worn by revolutionaries at the time. The tricolor was carried on the day of the storming of the Bastille in 1789, when political prisoners held there by the old regime were set free. Thus the tricolor is synonymous with the creation of the modern French Republic. The event is now celebrated each year on Bastille Day, on July 14.

Andorra

Capital city *Andorra La Vella*
Population *85,458*
Land area (sq. mi) *180;* **(sq. km)** *468*
Currency *1 euro = 100 cents*
Main languages *Catalan, French, Castilian*
Ratio 7:10

Situated between France and Spain, for centuries Andorra was jointly ruled by the French head of state and the Spanish bishop of Urgel. This unique dual system came to an end in 1993, when the government of the country became a modern parliamentary democracy. The blue, yellow, and red Andorran national flag reflects this history, with a coat of arms that displays two French quarters and two Spanish. The miter and the crozier of the Spanish bishop are on the top left-hand quarter, while two horned, red cows symbolizing the French province of Bearn are on the bottom right-hand quarter.

Monaco

Capital city *Monaco*
Population *36,370*
Land area (sq. mi) *0.75;* **(sq. km)** *1.95*
Currency *1 euro = 100 cents*
Languages *French, English, Italian, Monegasque*
Ratio 2:3

In the thirteenth century, the small principality of Monaco was acquired by a Genoese family, the house of Grimaldi. During the French Revolution, the Grimaldis lost the principality to France. It was later made part of the kingdom of Sardinia, but in 1861 was restored as an independent state to the French, who opened a large casino there. Today, the flag of Monaco displays the ancient heraldic colors of the Grimaldi: red and white. The current Monaco flag was officially adopted on April 4, 1881. Coincidentally, it is almost identical to the Indonesian flag, except that its proportions differ slightly.

Italy

The Italian flag, known as the tricolore, was inspired by the French flag that Napoleon brought to the country when he invaded it in 1796. However, instead of the blue band, a band of green is displayed. There are several possible explanations for the use of the green. It is thought that Bonaparte may have chosen it as the color of Corsica, or that it was copied from the uniforms of the city militia in Milan. The color green was also associated with Lombardy. Italy at that time was not a unified country, and did not become so until late in the nineteenth century. The design changed over the years, in accordance with the political upheavals of the times. The present flag was adopted in 1946, after World War II.

Capital city *Rome*
Population *61,680,122*
Land area (sq. mi) *116,347;* **(sq. km)** *301,340*
Currency *1 euro = 100 cents*
Languages *Italian, German, French, Slovene*
Ratio 2:3

The Holy See (Vatican City)

Capital city *Vatican City*

Population *921*

Land area (sq. mi) *0.17*; **(sq. km)** *0.44*

Currency *1 euro = 100 cents*

Languages *Italian, Latin, French*

Ratio 1:1

The Holy See is the independent state of the Vatican City, presided over by the Roman Catholic pope. For centuries, powerful popes ruled parts of Italy in a secular role, until their lands were seized in the mid-nineteenth century by the newly unified kingdom of Italy. In 1929, the Vatican City was granted independence, and the Holy See resurrected its original flag. This shows the traditional papal colors of yellow and white, with the papal miter and the crossed keys of St. Peter. The colors yellow and white are simplified forms of the gold and silver traditionally used to portray the keys, which have been an emblem of papal authority since earliest times. The flag's symbolism indicates the enduring importance of the pope and the Roman Catholic faith today.

Malta

Capital city *Valletta*
Population *412,655*
Land area (sq. mi) *122;* **(sq. km)** *316*
Currency *1 euro = 100 cents*
Languages *Maltese, English*

Ratio 2:3

 The white and red colors of the Maltese flag are thought to originate from the checkered flag of the Norman Hauteville family, who conquered Malta in 1090. Legend has it that when he departed, Count Roger of Hauteville cut a corner off of the family flag and gave it to the Maltese. Today, as well as the two bands of red and white, the Maltese flag also displays a George Cross, edged in red, which was awarded to the island by the British. The Cross commemorates the heroism of the Maltese people in support of Britain during World War II.

San Marino

Capital city *San Marino*
Population *32,742*
Land area (sq. mi) *24;* **(sq. km)** *61.2*
Currency *1 euro = 100 cents*
Language *Italian*

Ratio 3:4

 The small state of San Marino claims to be the oldest republic in the world. Founded in 301 A.D. by Marinus, a Christian stonemason, it is now closely allied with Italy. The flag's top band is white and the bottom is light blue. The national coat of arms sits in the center. This displays a shield with three towers on it, each topped by an ostrich feather, representing the three citadel towers of San Marino: Guaita, Cesta, and Montale. The crown above the shield symbolizes the republic's continuing independence and sovereignty, while a scroll below bears the word "Libertas" (Liberty).

Slovenia

Capital city *Ljubljana*

Population *2,011,473*

Land area (sq. mi) *7,827*; **(sq. km)** *20,273*

Currency *1 euro = 100 cents*

Languages *Slovenian, Serbo-Croatian*

Ratio 1:2

Slovenia's flag was adopted in 1991, when the country established its independence. (Before that date, the Slovenes, along with the Serbs and Croats, had been part of Yugoslavia.) The flag has three horizontal bands of white (top), blue (center), and red (bottom). On the upper hoist side, it displays the country's coat of arms, added in 1993. The white mountain on the coat of arms represents the snow-covered Mount Triglav, Slovenia's highest peak, while the two blue wavy lines stand for the country's rivers and seas. Above the mountain are three six-pointed stars in an inverted triangle, on a dark blue background. This image is taken from the coat of arms of the ancient house of Celje, which was a powerful Slovenian dynasty during the fourteenth and fifteenth centuries.

Croatia

Capital city *Zagreb*
Population *4,496,869*
Land area (sq. mi) *21,830;* **(sq. km)** *56,594*
Currency *1 kuna = 100 lipas*
Language *Croatian*

Ratio 1:2

Croatia has a history of bitter conflict over its territory, most recently with the Serbs after declaring its independence from Yugoslavia in 1991. As a result of these struggles, the national flag and its distinctive coat of arms have particular significance for its people. The Croatian flag displays a national coat of arms on a ground of three red, white, and blue horizontal bands. A large checkered shield denotes the nation of Croatia, while five smaller ones show the arms of the provinces: Old Croatia, with a silver crescent moon and a gold star; Dubrovnik, with two red stripes on a blue ground; Dalmatia, with three golden lion's heads; Istria, with a red-horned, red-hoofed golden goat; and Slavonica, with a black marten below a golden star and a red stripe.

Serbia

Capital city *Belgrade*

Population *7,209,764*

Land area (sq. mi) *29,912;* **(sq. km)** *77,474*

Currency *1 Serbian dinar = 100 para*

Languages *Serbian, Hungarian*

Ratio 2:3

After the breakup of the former Yugoslavia in the early 1990s, Serbia and Montenegro formed a federal republic. The union was dissolved in 2006, when both nations declared independence. The present flag includes the Serbian coat of arms, depicting the royal crown of the former monarchy. A central shield bears the Serbian cross, while the two-headed eagle derives from the Byzantine era, symbolizing the empire's rule over East and West. The flag has three equal horizontal bands, with red at the top, blue in the middle, and white at the bottom. The colors were adopted at the Pan-Slavic Congress in 1848, at a time when many Slavic people were under foreign dominion, and were drawn from the original Russian flag, which for many years was a symbol of hope for the Slavs.

Montenegro

Capital city *Podgorica*
Population *650,036*
Land area (sq. mi) *5,332;* **(sq. km)** *13,812*
Currency *1 euro = 100 cents*
Languages *Serbian, Montenegrin, Bosnian, Albanian*

Ratio 1:2

The state of Montenegro has a flag that looks back to its past. The double-headed eagle together with the lion on an escutcheon (shield) formed part of the arms of the royal Njegoš dynasty that ruled Montenegro from 1696 to 1918. The flag, which is red with a gold border, was adopted in 2004, when Montenegro was still in federation with Serbia. It became a national flag in 2006, when Montenegro voted to dissolve the federation with Serbia. Considering that it is the symbol of a new democratic republic, the flag looks distinctly old-fashioned and regal. But it has proved hugely popular with the Montenegrin population.

Albania

 The striking national flag of Albania displays a black two-headed eagle in the center of a red ground. Known as "Skanderbeg's flag," it dates from the fifteenth century, when an Albanian called George Kastrioti became a general in the Turkish army. He converted to Islam and adopted the name Skanderbeg, which derives from Iskander (a variant of Alexander, after Alexander the Great) and "bey," meaning "lord." After a very distinguished career, Skanderbeg abandoned the Turkish army in 1443 and returned home to Albania, where he raised the flag of the black, double-headed eagle over his father's castle at Kruja and proclaimed, "I have not brought you liberty, I found it here, among you." He went on to unite the Albanian provinces and defend Albania against repeated attacks by the Turks.

Capital city *Tirana*
Population *3,544,808*
Land area (sq. mi) *11,099;* **(sq. km)** *28,748*
Currency *1 lek = 100 qintars*
Languages *Albanian, Greek*

Ratio 5:7

Bosnia and Herzegovina

Capital city *Sarajevo*
Population *4,007,608*
Land area (sq. mi) *19,767;* **(sq. km)** *51,197*
Currency *1 marka = 100 fening*
Languages *Bosnian, Croatian, Serbian*

Ratio 1:2

Bosnia and Herzegovina's national flag has an unusual design of a yellow isosceles triangle on a blue ground. Along the side of the triangle are seven five-pointed white stars. At the top and bottom of the row are two half stars. The two half stars, if connected, would make one whole star. The flag, with its blue ground and white stars, is said to represent the Council of Europe, of which Bosnia and Herzegovina is a part. This politically and ethnically neutral design was adopted several years after Bosnia and Herzegovina's declaration of independence from the former Yugoslavia in 1992.

Macedonia

Capital city *Skopje*
Population *2,091,719*
Land area (sq. mi) *9,927;* **(sq. km)** *25,713*
Currency *1 denar = 100 deni*
Main languages *Macedonian, Albanian, Turkish*

Ratio 1:2

When the former Yugoslav Republic of Macedonia came into being the early 1990s, an open competition was held to design a flag for the new republic. The idea of a yellow sun on a red ground, to symbolize hope, was chosen. However, the initial design of a Vergina sun, with rays that narrow toward the end, was objected to by Greece on the grounds that it is a Hellenic symbol. (Others claim that it is found from earliest times in many ancient countries, including Persia.) Eventually, a yellow sun on a red ground with broadening rays was adopted in 1995.

Greece

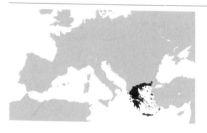

Capital city *Athens*

Population *10,775,557*

Land area (sq. mi) *50,948;* **(sq. km)** *131,957*

Currency *1 euro = 100 cents*

Language *Greek*

Ratio 2:3

The nine horizontal stripes on the Greek flag are generally held to stand for the nine syllables of the phrase "Eleftheria i Thanatos," meaning "Freedom or Death." This was the motto of the Greek patriots during the years of the Hellenic revolution against the Ottoman Empire, which took place during the nineteenth century. The white cross on the upper hoist side of the flag reflects the Greeks' respect for the Orthodox Church, which played an important role in maintaining the country's cultural identity during the years of occupation. The blue and white colors of the flag are thought to be reminiscent of the blue Aegean Sea, especially on a windy day when it is flecked with waves. The Greek national flag is known as the Galanolefci, which means "blue and white."

Bulgaria

Capital city *Sofia*

Population *7,517,973*

Land area (sq. mi) *42,810;* **(sq. km)** *110,879*

Currency *1 lev = 100 stotinki*

Language *Bulgarian*

Ratio 3:5

The flag of Bulgaria features three bands of color: white at the top, representing peace; green in the middle representing the land; and red at the bottom, representing the courage of the Bulgarian people. Originally, there was an emblem to the upper left of the flag showing a lion and a wreath of wheat under a red star, bearing the dates 681 and 1944. These were the dates that the first Bulgarian state was established, and the date that the country was liberated from the Nazis during World War II. In 1946, Bulgaria came under the influence of the Soviet regime and was established as a People's Republic. When this socialist regime came to an end in 1990, the emblem was removed and now only the three bands remain.

Romania

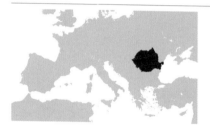

Capital city *Bucharest*

Population *22,355,551*

Land area (sq. mi) *92,042;* **(sq. km)** *238,391*

Currency *1 lei = 100 bani*

Languages *Romanian, Hungarian, German*

Ratio 2:3

Romania's flag is a vertical tricolor with three equal bands of blue, yellow, and red (from left to right). At various periods in its history, the flag has also featured an emblem in the center. In 1947, Romania became a People's Republic under the aegis of the Soviet Union. From 1965, the Communist regime became increasingly oppressive under dictator Nicolae Ceausescu, until he was overthrown and executed in 1989. During this period, the population took to displaying flags with the central emblem cut out of the middle, to show their disgust with the Communist regime. Eventually, this way of symbolizing Romania's break with the past was officially sanctioned, and the plain tricolor was reestablished. Unfortunately, this means that Romania's flag is now identical to that of Chad, an unrelated country.

Moldova

 The Moldovan flag shares its colors of blue, yellow, and red with that of Romania. Currently the poorest European country, Moldova nevertheless has a proud history, reflected in the central emblem of its national flag. This shows a golden eagle with a yellow cross in its beak, carrying a scepter in its left talon and an olive branch in its right. A shield on the eagle's breast displays the head of an auroch, a large prehistoric beast that survived in remote parts of Eastern Europe until the seventeenth century, when it became extinct. The auroch signifies power, independence, and pride.

Capital city *Chisinau*

Population *4,446,455*

Land area (sq. mi) *13,069;* **(sq. km)** *33,851*

Currency *1 lei = 100 bani*

Languages *Moldovan, Romanian, Russian*

Ratio 1:2

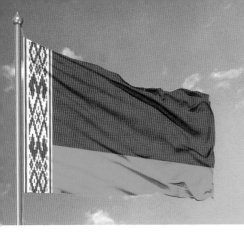

Belarus

Capital city *Minsk*

Population *10,310,520*

Land area (sq. mi) *80,154;* **(sq. km)** *207,600*

Currency *1 ruble = 100 kopeks*

Languages *Belarusian, Russian*

Ratio 1:2

Since it declared its independence from the Soviet Union in 1991, Belarus has maintained close ties with Russia. Today, its flag no longer bears the golden hammer and sickle, but now has two plain horizontal bands of red and green with a red-on-white vertical design at the hoist side. This design is known as the Belarus national ornament, and is said to symbolize the spiritual wealth, as well as the practical skills, of its people. It also makes reference to the ancient folk culture of the country. Patterns such as these are often used to decorate the Belarus national costume.

Ukraine

Capital city *Kiev*

Population *47,732,079*

Land area (sq. mi) *233,030;* **(sq. km)** *603,550*

Currency *1 hyrvnia = 100 kopiyka*

Languages *Ukrainian, Russian, Romanian, Polish, Hungarian*

Ratio 2:3

The simple blue and yellow horizontal bands of the Ukrainian flag tell a complex story. As Kievan Rus, this Slavic state was powerful in the tenth and eleventh century, but was later incorporated into Lithuania. It then reestablished its independence but became part of the Russian Empire, and eventually, of the USSR. Millions of Ukrainians died from famine and war during this period. In 1991, Ukraine became independent once more, but economic stability has proved difficult to achieve. As a result of this beleaguered history, the Ukrainian flag's colors of blue and yellow have a special significance for its people. Blue symbolizes its wide sky, while yellow represents its golden fields of corn. The colors also have a religious significance, dating from the introduction of Christianity to the region's people.

Russian Federation

Capital city *Moscow*

Population *143,782,338*

Land area (sq. mi) *6,601,637;* **(sq. km)** *17,098,242*

Currency *1 ruble = 100 kopecks*

Language *Russian*

Ratio 2:3

The Russian tricolor with its three equal horizontal bands of white, red, and blue was abandoned for many years under the Communist regime, which instead adopted the hammer and sickle. However, when the Soviet regime finally collapsed in 1991, the original tricolor, which had been the national flag before the revolution of 1917, was flown again—this time, over the Kremlin. Today, opinions as to the meaning of the three colors vary: some believe that the white traditionally stands for nobility, the blue for honesty, and the scarlet for courage; others that white is for the Belarusians, the blue for the Ukrainians, and the red for the Russians; or that the flag represents the old order, with God (white) over the Czar (blue), and the Czar over the people (red).

Poland

Capital city *Warsaw*
Population *38,626,349*
Land area (sq. mi) *120,727;* **(sq. km)** *312,685*
Currency *1 zloty = 100 groszy*
Language *Polish*

Ratio 5:8

The Polish national flag, with its two horizontal bands of red and white, has an ancient history dating back to the pennants of medieval times. In those days, the flag showed a white eagle on a red ground, and although the eagle was later removed, the colors of red and white came to symbolize the Polish national identity. At various times in Polish history, the colors were worn as ornaments; for example, in 1788, red and white ribbons were introduced. From the eighteenth century onward, Poland underwent a series of occupations, first by Russia, Prussia, and Austria, then by Germany, and finally by the Soviet Union. During these periods, the red and white national colors continued to hold a special significance for the Polish people, regardless of the regime in power.

Slovakia

Capital city *Bratislava*

Population *5,443,583*

Land area (sq. mi) *18,932;* **(sq. km)** *49,035*

Currency *1 euro = 100 cents*

Languages *Slovak, Hungarian*

Ratio 2:3

In 1918, the Slovaks united with the Czechs to form Czechoslovakia, which later came under Communist rule. After the collapse of the Soviet Union, the two countries separated peacefully in 1993. Today, the Slovakian flag displays a distinctive coat of arms on the center hoist side: a double Christian cross set over three hills, which signifies the arrival of Christianity to the region of the Carpathian Mountains. The cross is an ancient Slovakian emblem. The colors of the Slovakian flag were adopted in 1848, at a time when Slavs wished to unite in their fight for independence against the Austro-Hungarian Empire. The horizontal bands of white (top), blue (center), and red (bottom) derive from the Russian tricolor. This basic design is now found on the flags of many Eastern European countries.

Czech Republic

Capital city *Prague*
Population *10,627,448*
Land area (sq. mi) *30,450;* **(sq. km)** *78,867*
Currency *1 Czech koruna = 100 halers*
Language *Czech*

Ratio 2:3

The Czech flag consists of a blue triangle at the hoist side, intersecting two equal bands, one of white, and one of red. These three sections symbolize unity, an important concept for a country of which the national identity has constantly changed throughout history. In 1918, Bohemia and Moravia, inhabited by Czechs, were united with Slovakia and part of Silesia to make one state, Czechoslovakia. The new state broke up during World War II but was reestablished in 1945, when it came under Communist rule. In 1993, after the demise of the Soviet Union, Czechoslovakia split into two countries: the Czech Republic and Slovakia. Today, the Czech Republic retains the original Czechoslovakian flag, which displays the traditional Czech colors of red and white, together with the blue of the Bohemian flag.

Hungary

Capital city *Budapest*

Population *10,032,375*

Land area (sq. mi) *35,918;* **(sq. km)** *93,028*

Currency *1 forint = 100 filler*

Language *Hungarian*

Ratio 1:2

The Hungarian flag with its equal horizontal bands of red, white, and green, was first flown in 1848 during a national uprising against its Austrian rulers. The flag's design mirrors that of the French tricolor, which became a symbol of liberty during the French Revolution. However, the colors of the Hungarian flag date further back, to the ninth century, when Arpad, leader of the Magyars, adopted a plain red flag as his standard. In the tenth century, a cross on a white ground came to symbolize the country's conversion to Christianity. By the fifteenth century, green had been added to form the country's national colors, which can be seen on the flag today. The red is said to stand for strength, the white for faithfulness, and the green for hope.

Austria

Capital city *Vienna*
Population *8,223,062*
Land area (sq. mi) *32,382;* **(sq. km)** *83,871*
Currency *1 euro = 100 cents*
Languages *German, Slovene, Croatian, Hungarian*
Ratio 2:3

The Austrian flag consists of three equal horizontal bands of red (top), white (center), and red (bottom). The colors date back to the twelfth century. According to legend, the first Babenburg ruler of Austria, Duke Leopold V, fought in the Battle of Ptolemais in 1191. During the battle, he was wounded, and his tunic became so bloodstained that the only white part remaining was a band around his middle, which had been covered by his sword belt. As the battle continued, the duke lost his standard, so he raised his bloodied tunic up as a rallying point to his men. Later, in the thirteenth century, the last Babenburg ruler, Duke Friedrich II, adopted the red and white colors as his seal, as a mark of respect to his forebear.

Germany

Capital city *Berlin*

Population *82,424,609*

Land area (sq. mi) *137,846;* **(sq. km)** *357,022*

Currency *1 euro = 100 cents*

Language *German*

Ratio 3:5

The black, red, and yellow German tricolor has been adopted, abolished, and readopted several times in the country's history. In the mid-nineteenth century, the colors came to symbolize the aspirations of those wanting to unify the German states. In 1919, the tricolor was formally adopted as the flag of the Weimar Republic. In 1933, with the advent of the Third Reich, the tricolor was dropped and replaced by the Nazi swastika. After the defeat of the Nazis in World War II, the tricolor was raised once more, and became the modern German flag in 1949. During the period from 1959 to 1990, the East Germans flew a version of the tricolor with a Communist symbol on it, but this was taken off when the two Germanies were reunited.

Switzerland

Capital city *Bern*
Population *8,061,516*
Land area (sq. mi) *15,937;* **(sq. km)** *41,277*
Currency *1 Swiss franc = 100 centimes*
Languages *German, French, Italian, Romansch*

Ratio 1:1

 Switzerland's distinctive flag of a bold white cross on a red field dates back to medieval times, when it was part of the Holy Roman Empire. The white cross symbolizes the Christian cross, and the red ground stands for the blood of Christian martyrs. In the thirteenth century, the Swiss cantons of Schwyz, Uri, and Unterwalden banded together to form a league against the Holy Roman Emperor Rudolf I of the Habsburg dynasty; later, other cantons joined the league and eventually won their independence. Accordingly, the symbol of the Swiss white cross has come to be associated with independence and democracy. In modern times, Switzerland has consistently pursued a policy of neutrality in times of war; thus the flag has also come to stand for peace and refuge.

Liechtenstein

Capital city *Vaduz*
Population *37,313*
Land area (sq. mi) *62;* **(sq. km)** *160*
Currency *1 Swiss franc = 100 centimes*
Languages *German*, *Alemannic dialect*
Ratio 3:5

Liechtenstein was established as a principality in 1719 and became a state in 1806. It was closely allied to Austria until the end of World War I, when it moved toward economic union with Switzerland. Its flag has two horizontal bands of blue and red, with a gold crown on the top hoist side. The crown was added in 1937, and the new flag given the following official interpretation: "Blue is the color of the radiant sky, red the color of the embers in the fireplace during evening gatherings; gold…shows that our people…are united in heart and spirit."

Luxembourg

Capital city *Luxembourg*
Population *520,672*
Land area (sq. mi) *998;* **(sq. km)** *2,586*
Currency *1 euro = 100 cents*
Languages *Luxembourgish*, *German*, *French*
Ratio 3:5

Once part of the Holy Roman Empire, Luxembourg fell under Hapsburg rule before being overrun, at various times in its history, by Spain, Austria, France, and Belgium. Although Luxembourg became a grand duchy at the Congress of Vienna in 1815, it did not achieve independence until 1867. The colors of the Luxembourg flag, adopted in 1972, originate from the grand duchy's coat of arms, which features a red lion on a ground of blue and white stripes. The flag is similar to that of The Netherlands, except that the blue is a lighter shade, and the proportions are slightly different.

Netherlands

Capital city *Amsterdam*

Population *16,877,351*

Land area (sq. mi) *16,039;* **(sq. km)** *41,543*

Currency *1 euro = 100 cents*

Languages *Dutch, Frisian*

Ratio 2:3

The flag of the Netherlands was originally known as "the Prince's flag," after Prince William I of Orange, who led the country in a revolt against Spanish domination under the Hapsburg Empire in the sixteenth century. Prince William's flag was in fact orange, red, and white but changed to red, white, and blue in the mid-seventeenth century (possibly because red was easier to recognize at sea). The latter version of the flag is thought to have been the inspiration for the French tricolor, another important symbol of freedom and independence. Today, the flag of the Netherlands is one of the oldest flags to have survived intact throughout many changes in the country's history. Although orange no longer appears on the flag, it continues to be used as the country's national color.

Belgium

Capital city *Brussels*
Population *10,348,276*
Land area (sq. mi) *11,786;* **(sq. km)** *30,528*
Currency *1 euro = 100 cents*
Languages *Dutch, French, German*

Ratio 13:15

Adopted in 1831, the design of the Belgian flag, featuring three vertical bands, is based on the French tricolor. The distinctive colors of black, yellow, and red are thought to originate from the province of Brabant, which once extended over parts of what is now Belgium and the Netherlands. The Brabant coat of arms shows a yellow lion with a red tongue and claws, on a black ground. During the Brabant Revolt of 1787–89 against Austrian rule, these colors were displayed by the rebels. The revolt failed, but in 1830, the colors were raised again against William I of the Netherlands. This time, the rebellion was successful. Thus the Belgian flag, both in its design and in its colors, makes reference to the country's historic struggle for independence and liberty.

Denmark

Capital city *Copenhagen*
Population *5,569,077*
Land area (sq. mi) *16,383;* **(sq. km)** *42,434*
Currency *Danish krone = 100 ore*
Languages *Danish, Faroese, Greenlandic, German*
Ratio 28:37

The Danish flag is known as "Dannebrog," which means "The cloth of the Danes." The flag displays a white cross extending to the edges of the flag, set on a red ground. The vertical arm of the cross is toward the hoist side of the flag, in a design that has been repeated by other Scandinavian countries such as Norway and Sweden. Legend has it that the white cross on a red ground came down from heaven as a sign of divine approval to King Valdemar II before the Battle of Lyndanise against the pagan Estonians in 1219. With the flag in hand, the king was able to win the battle. Today, the national square-ended flag is cut into a swallow-tail shape to become the state flag and naval ensign.

Lithuania

Capital city *Vilnius*

Population *3,607,899*

Land area (sq. mi) *25,212;* **(sq. km)** *65,300*

Currency *1 euro = 100 cents*

Languages *Lithuanian, Russian, Polish*

Ratio 3:5

From 1918 to 1940 Lithuania's national flag was the tricolor of yellow, green, and red. In 1940, the country became part of the USSR and the old flag was dropped. In 1989, Lithuania broke away from the USSR and the tricolor was revived as the national flag once more. (The proportions of the new flag differ slightly from the original, however.) The yellow at the top is said to stand for the country's fields of grain; the green in the center for its forests; and the red at the bottom for the blood shed by its people to defend their nation.

Latvia

Capital city *Riga*

Population *2,306,306*

Land area (sq. mi) *24,937;* **(sq. km)** *64,589*

Currency *1 euro = 100 cents*

Languages *Latvian, Russian*

Ratio 1:2

Legend has it that the dark red color of the Latvian flag comes from its early history, when tribes used juice to make crimson dye for their battle standard. The narrow white band of the flag is said to stand for justice, truth, and honor, while the red on either side represents the blood shed by its citizens in pursuit of freedom. During the period of Communist rule in Latvia the flag was declared illegal, but was flown in defiance of the regime, and officially replaced the Soviet Latvian flag in 1991, when the country once more became independent.

Estonia

Capital city *Tallinn*

Population *1,341,664*

Land area (sq. mi) *17,462;* **(sq. km)** *45,226*

Currency *1 euro = 100 cents*

Languages *Estonian, Russian, Ukrainian, Finnish*

Ratio 7:11

The Estonian flag is a horizontal tricolor of cornflower blue (top), black (center), and white. The blue is said to symbolize the sea, sky, and lakes of the country, and is also said to be the color of fidelity. The black band echoes the traditional black jacket worn by Estonian peasants in the past, and is also a reminder of the suffering of the Estonian people, who for centuries were ruled by oppressive foreign powers. The white band calls to mind the snow that covers Estonia for many months of the year, and is also thought to represent the people's wish for freedom. An early symbol of nationalism, the flag was banned from 1940 to 1990 under the Soviet regime, but was flown once more when Estonia became independent.

Finland

Capital city *Helsinki*

Population *5,268,799*

Land area (sq. mi) *130,557;* **(sq. km)** *338,145*

Currency *1 euro = 100 cents*

Languages *Finnish, Swedish*

Ratio 11:18

Like the Danish "Dannebrog," the Finnish flag displays a large cross, extending to the edges of the flag, with the vertical arm shifted toward the hoist side. This design is used by many of the Nordic countries, and is known as "the Scandinavian cross." However, the design and color of the Finnish flag is distinctive, the cross being wide and solid, and featuring the color blue on a white ground. The origins of the cross are enshrined in Nordic legends, but in modern times the Finnish version of it, with the blue cross on a white ground, was adopted at the close of World War I, when the country won its independence. The blue is said to stand for the country's many lakes, while the white represents its snowy landscape.

Sweden

Capital city *Stockholm*

Population *9,723,809*

Land area (sq. mi) *173,859;* **(sq. km)** *450,295*

Currency *1 Swedish krone = 100 ore*

Language *Swedish*

Ratio 5:8

The design of the Swedish flag is probably related to that of the Danish "Dannebrog." The cross extending to each edge of the flag, with the vertical arm towards the hoist side, also occurs in other Nordic flag designs, such as the Finnish, Norwegian, and Icelandic national flags. The distinctive blue and yellow colors of the Swedish flag date back to the fourteenth century, and are thought to come from the country's ancient coat of arms, which features three golden crowns on a blue ground. Records show that the flag was used from the sixteenth century, when it was decreed that the yellow cross should always be borne on Swedish battle standards and banners. However, the present version of the flag was not officially adopted until 1906.

Norway

Capital city *Oslo*
Population *4,574,560*
Land area (sq. mi) *125,020;* **(sq. km)** *323,802*
Currency *1 Norwegian krone = 100 ore*
Languages *Bokmal Norwegian, Nynorsk Norwegian*
Ratio 8:11

The off-centered cross of the Norwegian flag, known as the Scandinavian cross, shows its links to the other Nordic countries, many of which use different versions of the same design. For more than four centuries, Norway was ruled by Denmark, and after that by Sweden, only achieving complete independence in the early twentieth century. During World War II, Norway proclaimed itself neutral, but was occupied by Nazi Germany until 1945. Its national flag, designed by Frederik Meltzer in 1821 and adopted in 1898, reflects the country's historical connections to Denmark, with the white cross on a red ground, and to Sweden, with the blue cross outlined by the white. The colors also make reference to Norway's desire for independence, echoing the red, white, and blue of the French tricolor.

Iceland

Capital city *Reykjavik*

Population *317,351*

Land area (sq. mi) *39,768;* **(sq. km)** *103,000*

Currency *1 Icelandic krone = 100 ore*

Languages *Icelandic, English, Nordic languages*

Ratio 5:7

Iceland has a distinguished place in European history as the first country to hold a parliament, the Althing, in the year 930. For centuries, Iceland was ruled by Norway, and then by Denmark. During this period, the population declined rapidly, as many of its people migrated or died from disease. In 1918, Iceland gained a measure of independence from the Danish as a separate realm within the kingdom of Denmark, and adopted a new flag. The flag featured the off-centred Scandinavian cross in red, bordered by white, on a blue field. Matthias Thordarson, the flag's designer, explained that the red stood for Iceland's many active volcanoes, the white for its icy landscape, and the blue for its mountains. On achieving full independence in 1944, the nation adopted it as the official flag.

Faroe Islands

Capital city *Torshavn*
Population *49,947*
Land area (sq. mi) *537;* **(sq. km)** *1,393*
Currency *1 Danish krone = 100 ore*
Languages *Faroese, Danish*

Ratio 8:11

The flag of the Faroe Islands displays the Scandinavian cross as a symbol of its historic links to Norway and Denmark. After Viking settlers arrived there in the ninth century, the islands were ruled for centuries by Norway and Denmark. The Faroe Islands are still part of the kingdom of Denmark, but since the mid 1940s they have been largely self-governing. The national flag was adopted in 1948. It shows the red and white colors of Denmark, but in reverse with a red cross on a white ground. The cross is edged in blue, which recalls the Norwegian flag.

Greenland

Capital city *Nuuk (Godthab)*
Population *57,728*
Land area (sq. mi) *836,326;* **(sq. km)** *2,166,086*
Currency *Danish krone = 100 ore*
Languages *Greenlandic, Danish, English*

Ratio 2:3

Greenland is the world's largest island, and was settled by Native Americans before Europeans arrived there. Later ruled by Norway and then by Denmark, it became self-governing in 1979. Its flag, adopted in 1985, was designed by Thue Christiansen. According to Christiansen, the white band symbolizes Greenland's ice cap, and the red upper circle represents its fjords. The red band on the lower half of the flag symbolizes the ocean, and the white lower circle represents icebergs and pack ice. Another impression the design creates is of a far-northern sunrise or sunset over ice.

Ireland

Capital city *Dublin*
Population *4,832,765*
Land area (sq. mi) *27,132;* **(sq. km)** *70,273*
Currency *1 euro = 100 cents*
Languages *English, Irish (Gaelic)*

Ratio 1:2

The tricolor of Ireland dates back to 1848, when the Young Ireland movement, a nationalist organization, flew the flag in defiance of British rule. By 1916, at the time of the Easter Rising when Irish nationalists declared independence, the green, white, and orange tricolor had come into popular use. In 1920, it became the national flag, replacing the older Green Flag of Ireland, which showed a gold harp on a green ground. As well as making reference to the French tricolor as a symbol of liberty, the Irish flag represents the two main religious and political groups of Ireland: green for the Catholics and orange for the Protestants. The white band in the center of the flag apparently represents the hope of lasting peace between these two—often polarized—communities.

United Kingdom

Capital city *London*
Population *63,742,977*
Land area (sq. mi) *94,525;* **(sq. km)** *243,610*
Currency *1 pound = 100 pence*
Languages *English, Welsh, Scottish Gaelic*
Ratio 1:2

The national flag of the United Kingdom reflects the links between England, Scotland, and Ireland. The red cross of St. George, the patron saint of England, is edged in white on a blue field. The diagonal white cross, or saltire, of St. Andrew (patron saint of Scotland) is also shown. Set within it is the saltire of St. Patrick (patron saint of Ireland). The formal name of the flag is the Union Flag, but it is generally known as the Union Jack. The flag came into use when James VI, the Scottish king, also became King of England in 1603. In 1801, Ireland joined the union, and the Irish saltire was added. The Union Jack appears on many flags around the world, recalling Britain's global empire during the nineteenth century.

England

Capital city *London*
Population *53,012,456*
Land area (sq. mi) *50,356;* **(sq. km)** *130,423*
Currency *1 pound = 100 pence*
Language *English*

Ratio 3:5

The flag of England is the St. George's Cross, which consists of a red cross on a white background. The flag was first adopted by the English king Richard the Lionheart on his crusades to the Holy Land in the twelfth century, in honor of St. George. St. George was a Christian born in the year 270 A.D. who became a soldier in the Roman army and was eventually beheaded when he refused to give up his faith. Many years later, in 1415, he was declared the patron saint of England. Today, the flag of St. George makes up part of the Union Flag, or Union Jack, of the United Kingdom. In recent years, it has resurfaced in its original form as a popular emblem for England supporters at soccer games.

Scotland

Capital city *Edinburgh*

Population *5,327,700*

Land area (sq. mi) *30,420;* **(sq. km)** *78,789*

Currency *1 pound = 100 pence*

Languages *English, Scottish Gaelic*

Ratio 3:5

The Scottish flag is the Cross of St. Andrew, consisting of a white diagonal cross, or saltire, on a blue ground. It is thought to date back to the twelfth century. Legend has it that St. Andrew, a Christian apostle, was put to death by the Romans by being crucified on a diagonal cross, and that many years afterward, his remains were taken to Scotland. The Cross of St. Andrew now makes up part of the Union Flag, or Union Jack, of the United Kingdom, along with the Cross of St. George (for England) and the Cross of St. Patrick (for Ireland).

Wales

Capital city *Cardiff*

Population *3,063,456*

Land area (sq. mi) *8,023;* **(sq. km)** *20,779*

Currency *1 pound = 100 pence*

Languages *English, Welsh*

Ratio 3:5

The Welsh flag was officially adopted in 1958, but has been an ancient symbol of Wales for centuries. The Red Dragon was first brought to Britain by the Romans, and was later used by Saxon kings. In the twelfth century, it became the standard of Cadwalladr, a Welsh prince from whom the Tudor kings of England were descended. The two equal horizontal bands of white and green behind the dragon are the traditional livery colors of the Tudor dynasty. When Henry VII became King of England in 1485, he decreed that the Red Dragon should be used on the flag of Wales.

Jersey

Capital city *St. Helier*
Population *96,513*
Land area (sq. mi) *45;* **(sq. km)** *116*
Currency *1 pound = 100 pence*
Languages *English, Portuguese, local dialect*
Ratio 3:5

Jersey is the largest and most southerly of the Channel islands, and today is a dependency of the British crown. Its flag is a diagonal red cross, or saltire, against a white ground. In the upper half of the flag is a red shield with three yellow lions depicted on it. Over this is a yellow crown, with a shape recognizable as the crown of the Plantaganet kings. This design dates back to a royal seal that was given to the island in 1279 by Edward I. The current Jersey flag was officially hoisted for the first time in 1981.

Guernsey

Capital city *St. Peter Port*
Population *65,849*
Land area (sq. mi) *30;* **(sq. km)** *78*
Currency *1 pound = 100 pence*
Languages *English, French, local dialect*
Ratio 2:3

The flag of Guernsey, one of the major Channel Islands, has ancient connections with the Normans, who held sway in France and Britain in medieval times. The flag consists of a red cross on a white ground, which is the Cross of St. George, the patron saint of England. Within the red cross is a gold or yellow cross with equal arms and square ends, which appears on the Bayeux tapestry as the emblem of William the Conqueror, who invaded Britain in 1066. The gold cross was added to Guernsey's flag in 1985, to distinguish it from the English flag.

Sark

Capital city *none*
Population *600*
Land area (sq. mi) *2;* **(sq. km)** *5.5*
Currency *1 pound = 100 pence*
Languages *English, French, local dialect*

Ratio 3:5

The Channel Island of Sark comprises Great Sark and Little Sark, two land areas connected by an isthmus. In French, the island is known as "Serq." Its flag shows the St. George's cross, a red cross on a white ground. On the upper hoist side is a red canton with two yellow lions. This design is derived from the arms of the house of Normandy, which has strong historical links to the island. The Sark flag was originally that of the Seigneur or governor of Sark, but became the island flag in the 1980s, at the suggestion of the Seigneur.

Alderney

Capital city *St. Anne*
Population *2,400*
Land area (sq. mi) *24;* **(sq. km)** *62*
Currency *1 pound = 100 pence*
Languages *English, French, local dialect*

Ratio 1:2

Alderney is the third largest of the Channel Islands, and lies only 8 miles (13 km) away from the coast of France. Its flag, like that of other Channel Islands, is based on the St. George's Cross. This features a red cross on a white ground, and has since ancient times been used as the English flag. Alderney's flag is distinguishable from its neighbors by a green disk in the center, which displays a crowned golden lion bearing a sprig of leaves. The disk has a gold border. Below the shield is the legend "Riduna," which was the Roman name for Alderney.

Isle of Man

Capital city *Douglas*
Population *84,497*
Land area (sq. mi) *221;* **(sq. km)** *572*
Currency *1 pound = 100 pence*
Languages *English, Manx Gaelic*

Ratio 1:2

The Isle of Man flag shows an ancient symbol of three legs joined at the thigh and bent at the knee. This is known as the "trinacria" and has been found at different times and in different cultures throughout human history, for example, in prehistoric Italian rock carvings, in ancient Greek art, and in Norse mythology. According to legend, the feet on the legs must point clockwise, or the symbol is deemed to have an evil intent. So as to have the toes pointing in the right direction on each side of the island's flag, a double-sided emblem is used.

Gibraltar

Capital city *Gibraltar*
Population *29,185*
Land area (sq. mi) *2.5;* **(sq. km)** *6.5*
Currency *1 Gibraltar pound = 100 pence*
Main Languages *English, Spanish, Italian*

Ratio 1:2

Gibraltar has a distinctive flag, showing a three-towered red castle against a double band of white and a single band of red. Hanging from the castle is a large golden key, centered in the red band. The design of the flag represents Gibraltar's strategic importance throughout history. It dates back to 1501, when Queen Isabella of Spain granted Gibraltar its coat of arms. Up until 1713, Gibraltar was a Spanish territory, and was then ceded to Great Britain; it remains a British dependency. Gibraltar's official flag is the Union Jack, but citizens often use this coat of arms instead.

ASIA

The cultural diversity and complexity of the Asian continent
is reflected in the national flags of its countries. An ancient
symbol often encountered on Asian flags is the crescent
moon, often in conjunction with a single star. This has for many
centuries been used as a symbol of the Islamic faith, as has the
color green, which is also seen on the flags of many Muslim
countries. Among the Arab nations, the colors red, black, white,
and green, which date back to the early founding dynasties of
the Arab peoples, are also often used. In the countries of the
Far East, another ancient symbol, that of the full moon or "sun
circle" often appears, as on the flags of Laos and Japan. In
contrast, the twentieth-century Communist star on a red field
is also often seen on the flags of Asian countries, as a result
of the influence of China.

Turkey

Capital city *Ankara*

Population *81,619,392*

Land area (sq. mi) *302,533;* **(sq. km)** *783,562*

Currency *1 Turkish lira = 100 kurus*

Languages *Turkish, Kurdish, Arabic, Armenian, Greek*

Ratio 2:3

The flag of Turkey features a white crescent moon and a white star on a red ground. Both the color and the symbols have an ancient history. Red has been associated with the Ottoman Empire since its inception in the late thirteenth century. The moon and star are both traditional Islamic symbols, but are thought to predate Islam in Turkey. The moon was the symbol of Diana, the goddess of Byzantium. The star is associated with the Virgin Mary, to whom the city was rededicated when its name was changed to Constantinople. (Later, the city became Istanbul.) Legend has it that Sultan Murad II saw the moon and the star in a pool of blood at the Battle of Kosovo in 1448, and chose the symbols for the national flag.

Cyprus

Capital city *Nicosia*
Population *1,172,458*
Land area (sq. mi) *3,571;* **(sq. km)** *9,250*
Currency *1 euro = 100 cents*
Languages *Greek, Turkish, English*

Ratio 2:3

 The flag of Cyprus shows a map of the island in a yellow color, which refers to its copper deposits. (The name Cyprus is derived from the Greek word for copper.) Below it are two green olive branches, crossed at the stems. The olive branches represent the hope that the Greek and Turkish Cypriot communities will eventually live in peace. After achieving independence from Britain in 1960, conflicts arose and Turkish Cypriots declared part of the island a republic, adopting a flag showing a white field with a red crescent star and moon; however, this is not internationally recognized.

Armenia

Capital city *Yerevan*
Population *3,060,631*
Land area (sq. mi) *11,483;* **(sq. km)** *29,743*
Currency *1 dram = 100 lumas*
Languages *Armenian, Kurdish*

Ratio 1:2

 Armenia was the first nation to formally adopt Christianity in the fourth century. Since then, its history has been marked by conflict, as it became part of the Roman, Byzantine, Arab, Persian, and Ottoman Empires. In the twentieth century it became part of the USSR. The colors of the Armenian national flag are as follows: red for the spilled blood of Armenian soldiers, both past and present; blue for the sky, and for hope; orange for the fertile land and the people. The Armenian flag was adopted in 1990, but the colors date back as far as the second century.

Syria

Capital city *Damascus*
Population *17,951,639*
Land area (sq. mi) *71,498;* **(sq. km)** *185,180*
Currency *1 Syrian pound = 100 piastres*
Languages *Arabic, Kurdish, Armenian, Aramaic*
Ratio 2:3

The national flag of Syria shows the colors of black, white, red, and green. These were the colors adopted in the early twentieth century by the Pan-Arab movement in its fight for independence against the Ottoman Empire. After the breakup of the empire during World War I, Syria was governed by France until it achieved independence in 1946. Since then, its flag has changed several times, but today still carries the same colors, which continue to symbolize solidarity between the Arab nations. The present flag was first adopted in 1958 when Syria and Egypt became the United Arab Republic; later, as other political alliances were formed, another star was added; and then the stars were replaced with the symbol of a hawk. The original two-starred 1958 flag was readopted in 1980.

Lebanon

Capital city *Beirut*

Population *5,882,562*

Land area (sq. mi) *4,015;* **(sq. km)** *10,400*

Currency *1 Lebanese pound = 100 piastres*

Languages *Arabic, French, English, Armenian*

Ratio 2:3

"The righteous flourish like the palm tree, and grow like a cedar in Lebanon" (Psalm 92:12). Since biblical times, the cedar of Lebanon has been a Christian symbol of peace and prosperity. Today, its distinctive shape is represented in green at the center of the country's national flag, on a white ground flanked by two red bands at the top and bottom. The white, green, and red colors of the flag, which was adopted when Lebanon became independent in 1943, show the country's friendship with other Arab nations. White is said to stand for peace and for Lebanon's snow-capped mountains, while red symbolizes the blood shed in the country's struggle for liberation.

Israel

Capital city *Jerusalem*

Population *7,821,850*

Land area (sq. mi) *8,019;* **(sq. km)** *20,770*

Currency *1 shekel = 100 agorot*

Languages *Hebrew, Arabic*

Ratio 8:11

At the center of the Israeli national flag is a six-pointed blue star made from two triangles, known as the "Star of David." This flag design is over seven hundred years old, and derives from the Magen David, or Shield of David. The design is also known as "the Seal of Solomon," as it was also found on the ring of King Solomon. The two horizontal stripes of blue above and below the star, on a white ground, come from the pattern of the Jewish prayer shawl, or "tallith." The design of the flag has its origins in the Zionist movement of the late nineteenth century, which sought to create a Jewish homeland in Palestine, and was adopted as the national flag when the State of Israel was established in 1948.

Jordan

Capital city *Amman*

Population *7,930,491*

Land area (sq. mi) *34,494*; **(sq. km)** *89,342*

Currency *1 dinar = 1,000 fulus*

Language *Arabic*

Ratio 1:2

The colors of the Jordanian flag are those of the powerful Arab dynasties that go back to the medieval period. The black band at the top of the flag stands for the Abbasid dynasty of Baghdad; the white band in the center represents the Umayyad dynasty of Damascus; and the green band at the bottom stands for the Fatimid dynasty of Morocco. Intersecting the bands is a crimson triangle, which represents the Hashemite dynasty of Jordan. The white star on the crimson triangle has seven points, symbolizing the "Fatiha," the seven opening verses of the Koran. In 1916, these colors were raised by Hussein ibn Ali during the Arab revolt against the Ottoman Empire. In 1921, the present flag was adopted, but without a star; the star was added in 1928.

Bahrain

Capital city *Manama*
Population *1,314,089*
Land area (sq. mi) *293;* **(sq. km)** *760*
Currency *1 dinar = 1,000 fils*
Languages *Arabic, English, Farsi, Urdu*

Ratio 3:5

The national flag of Bahrain is red with a white stripe on the hoist side. The stripe has a striking serrated edge forming five triangles, which are said to represent the Five Pillars of Islam. Red is the traditional color of the Kharijite Muslims in eastern Arabia. The white stripe was added in 1820, when Britain asked all friendly Arab states to display a white border on the flags of ships. The aim of this was to prevent piracy in the Persian Gulf, which had long been a problem there. The present-day flag of Bahrain was officially adopted in 1932.

Kuwait

Like many other Arab countries, the national flag of Kuwait features the pan-Arab colors of black, white, red, and green, adopted at the end of World War I when Arab nationalists rose up against the Turkish Ottoman Empire (of which Kuwait was once a part). The green, white, and red bands are flanked on the hoist side by a black trapezoid. According to a well-known Arab poem, green stands for fertility, white for peace, red for chivalry, and black for battlefields. Black is also said to stand for the sand whirled by Kuwaiti horsemen in their fight for freedom.

Capital city *Kuwait*

Population *2,742,711*

Land area (sq. mi) *6,880;* **(sq. km)** *17,820*

Currency *1 Kuwaiti dinar = 1,000 fils*

Languages *Arabic, English*

Ratio 1:2

Saudi Arabia

Capital city *Riyadh*

Population *27,345,986*

Land area (sq. mi) *829,996;* **(sq. km)** *2,149,690*

Currency *1 riyal = 100 dirhams*

Language *Arabic*

Ratio 2:3

"There is no God but Allah, and Muhammad is the Prophet of Allah." Thus reads the inscription in Arabic script on the Saudi Arabian flag. Underneath the inscription, known as the "shahada" or Muslim creed, is a sword, pointing toward the hoist side of the flag. In the making of the flag, two reversed versions of the design are sewn back to back, so that the inscription reads properly on either side and the sword points the right way. The image of the sword commemorates the military victories of Ibn Saud, who unified the kingdom we now know as Saudi Arabia in the early twentieth century. Green is the traditional color of Islam, and especially of the Wahhabi and Sunni Muslims, who today form the religious majority in Saudi Arabia.

Yemen

Capital city *Sanaa*
Population *26,052,966*
Land area (sq. mi) *203,849;* **(sq. km)** *527,970*
Currency *1 Yemeni rial = 100 fils*
Language *Arabic*

Ratio 2:3

The current national flag of Yemen was adopted in 1990, when the North and South united to form a Republic. Prior to that time, the country had been divided into two states, the People's Democratic Republic of Yemen in the south, and the Yemen Arab Republic in the north. The southern state was a secular one, which had a flag showing a blue triangle and red star at the hoist side, while the Islamic northern state displayed a green star in the central band. When the two states united, these symbols were dropped, suggesting that the two countries had reached a compromise. What was left was the red, white, and black tricolor, in three equal horizontal bands. These colors are a symbol of the pan-Arab ideal of unity between Arab countries.

United Arab Emirates

Capital city *Abu Dhabi*

Population *5,628,805*

Land area (sq. mi) *32,000;* **(sq km)** *82,880*

Currency *1 dirham = 100 fils*

Languages *Arabic, Persian, English, Hindi, Urdu*

Ratio 1:2

The flag of the United Arab Emirates has a vertical red band on the hoist side, red being the traditional color of the Kharijite peoples of southeastern Arabia. The band of white in the center of the flag is familiar from the flags used in the Gulf area after 1820, when a Maritime Treaty was signed with Britain. The treaty required friendly states to display a white stripe on their flags so as to distinguish them from pirate ships. In 1971, the sheikdoms banded together to form one country, the United Arab Emirates, and adopted a national flag showing the Pan-Arab colors of red, green, white, and black, which stand for unity between the Arab nations. The colors also echo the flags of red and white that the sheikdoms used in the past.

Oman

Capital city *Muscat*
Population *3,219,775*
Land area (sq. mi) *119,498;* **(sq. km)** *309,500*
Currency *1 Omani rial = 1,000 baizas*
Languages *Arabic, English, Baluchi, Urdu*
Ratio 1:2

Like many other Arab states, the Omani national flag displays the red, white, and green colors that stand for unity between Arab peoples. In addition, on the upper hoist side, the Sultanate's arms appear in white on a red ground. The arms show two crossed sabers, a dagger, and a belt. The original Omani flag was a monochrome red, but in 1970, white and green panels in the upper and lower parts of the fly were added. According to the Oman Ministry of Information, the white is for peace, the red is for battles, and the green is for fertility.

Qatar

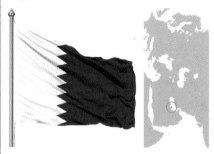

Capital city *Doha*
Population *2,123,160*
Land area (sq. mi) *4,415;* **(sq. km)** *11,586*
Currency *1 Qatari rial = 100 dirhams*
Language *Arabic*
Ratio 11:28

The national flag of Qatar is similar to that of Bahrain, but not identical. On the Qatari flag, the serrated edge of the vertical white stripe on the hoist side has nine points rather than five. To further distinguish it from Bahrain's flag, the color of the main part of the flag is maroon rather than red. The ratio of the flag is also entirely different. The maroon color of the flag is said to replicate the action of the hot Qatari sun on bright red cloth. The flag was officially adopted in 1971, the year when Qatar became fully independent.

Iraq

Capital city *Baghdad*
Population *32,585,692*
Land area (sq. mi) *169,234;* **(sq. km)** *438,317*
Currency *1 new Iraqi dinar = 1,000 fils*
Languages *Arabic, Kurdish, Assyrian, Armenian*
Ratio 2:3

The Pan-Arab colors of red, white, black, and green, which stand for unity between Arab peoples, are present on the Iraqi flag, as they are on the flags of many Arab nations. Here, they take the form of three bands of color (red at the top, white in the center, and black at the bottom), with an inscription in green on the center band. The colors date back to the early twentieth century, when Arab nationalists sought independence from the Ottoman Empire. Originally, the flag featured three stars representing the tenets of the former Ba'ath Party motto—unity, freedom, and socialism—however, these were removed when the flag was redesigned in 2008. The inscription, which was added during the 1991 Gulf War, reads "Allah-o-Akbar," meaning "God is Great."

Iran

Capital city *Tehran*

Population *80,840,713*

Land area (sq. mi) *636,293;* **(sq. km)** *1,648,195*

Currency *1 Iranian rial = 100 fils*

Languages *Persian, Turkic, Kurdish, Luri, Balochi, Arabic, Turkish*

Ratio 4:7

The red, green, and white colors of the Iranian flag are traditional, and are said to represent the Islamic religion (green), the hope for peace (white), and courage in battle (red). In 1907, the tricolor became the country's national flag. In 1979, the shah of Iran was overthrown and Iran became an Islamic republic. The national flag's original emblem, of a lion with a sword standing in front of a rising sun, was dropped. A new religious emblem was added, showing a stylized red tulip, which represents martyrdom. The design has five parts, standing for the five precepts of Islam, and the emblem as a whole also stands for "Allah." Along the borders of the green and white bands is the legend "God is Great," written in ancient Kufic script.

Azerbaijan

Capital city *Baku*

Population *9,686,210*

Land area (sq. mi) *33,436;* **(sq. km)** *86,600*

Currency *1 Azerbaijani manat = 100 gopiks*

Languages *Azerbaijani, Russian, Armenian*

Ratio 1:2

The symbol of a crescent moon and a star on the Azerbaijani national flag is an Islamic one. In this case, the eight points on the star represent the eight Turkic groups of Azerbaijan. The colors of the flag are also symbolic: the top band of light blue represents the unity of Turkic peoples; the central band of red stands for progress; and the green band at the bottom refers to the Muslim religion. The flag was first adopted in 1918, but was dropped during the Soviet regime; in 1991, when Azerbaijan regained independence, the flag was raised once more.

Georgia

Capital city *Tbilisi*

Population *4,935,880*

Land area (sq. mi) *26,911;* **(sq. km)** *69,700*

Currency *1 Georgian lari = 100 tetri*

Languages *Georgian, Russian, Armenian, Azeri*

Ratio 2:3

The new flag of the Republic of Georgia was adopted on January 14, 2004. It features a large red cross on a white ground, reaching to each edge of the flag. Within each quarter of the flag are four smaller red crosses. The flag appears to date back to the fourteenth century, when an unknown Franciscan monk wrote of "a white-colored cloth with five red crosses." The design is thought to relate to the Jerusalem cross, used by crusaders in the Holy Land, at a time when Georgians founded several early monasteries and became known for their religious piety.

Afghanistan

Capital city *Kabul*
Population *31,822,848*
Land area (sq. mi) *251,826;* **(sq. km)** *652,230*
Currency *1 Afghani = 100 puls*
Main languages *Dari, Pashto Turkic languages, Balochi, Pashai*

Ratio 2:3

Afghanistan's geopolitical significance has made it a fiercely contested region. No other flag since the beginning of the twentieth century has changed so often. The design derives from an earlier national flag flown between 1930 and 1973. It is a tricolor with a band of black (hoist side), red (center), and green (fly side). The black originally stood for the Abbasid caliphate, while the red denoted royalty; the green (fly side) continues to be associated with Islam. In the central red band is a gold or yellow emblem featuring the insignia of the "mihrab," the niche in a mosque where the person leading the congregation stands, and the "minbar," the pulpit from which the congregation are addressed. The insignia is encircled by a wreath, with the Islamic inscription "God is Great" above it.

Kyrgyzstan

Capital city *Bishkek*

Population *5,604,212*

Land area (sq. mi) *77,201;* **(sq. km)** *199,951*

Currency *1 Kyrgyzstani som = 100 tyiyn*

Languages *Kyrgyz, Russian, Uzbek*

Ratio 3:5

The yellow sun on the flag of Kyrgyzstan has 40 rays, representing the country's 40 tribes. According to legend, these tribes united together under Manas the Noble, the country's national hero, to form the nation. In the center of the sun is a stylized representation of the roof or "tunduk" of a yurt, the traditional tent used by the peoples of the steppes. The yellow sun is set on a red ground, red being the color of Manas's banner in ancient times. The flag was adopted in 1992, after the breakup of the USSR, of which Kyrgyzstan was a part.

Kazakhstan

Capital city *Astana*

Population *17,948,816*

Land area (sq. mi) *1,052,084;* **(sq. km)** *2,724,900*

Currency *1 tenge = 100 tyin*

Languages *Kazakh, Russian*

Ratio 1:2

In 1992, after the demise of the USSR, Kazakhstan became independent once more and celebrated its new freedom by adopting a new flag. This features a ground of sky blue, a traditional color of the nomadic peoples of Central Asia. This color was also used on the country's previous national flag. The current flag displays a gold pattern on the hoist side, which is officially described as "the national ornamentation." In the center of the flag is a golden sun with thirty-two rays. Flying below it is a species of eagle known in Kazakhstan as the "berkut," or steppe eagle.

Pakistan

 Pakistan's flag emphasizes the country's Muslim status with a white crescent moon and a five-pointed star on a dark green field. The moon and star are traditional Muslim symbols: the crescent denotes progress, while the star stands for knowledge and light. Green is also a traditional Islamic color. A white band on the hoist side of the flag is said to represent the country's non-Muslim minorities; together, the white and the green stand for peace and prosperity. The flag is based on that of the All-India Muslim League, which agitated for a separate Muslim state before 1947, when British India won independence from Britain and was partitioned into two nations, the largely Hindu India and the majority Muslim Pakistan. Later, after a civil war, East Pakistan became the separate nation of Bangladesh.

Capital city *Islamabad*

Population *196,174,380*

Land area (sq. mi) *307,372;* **(sq. km)** *796,095*

Currency *1 Pakistani rupee = 100 paise*

Main languages *Punjabi, Sindhi, Siraiki, Pashtu, Urdu, English*

Ratio 2:3

Tajikistan

Capital city *Dushanbe*
Population *8,051,512*
Land area (sq. mi) *55,251;* **(sq. km)** *143,100*
Currency *1 somoni = 100 diram*
Languages *Tajik, Russian*

Ratio 1:2

The national flag of Tajikistan, a former Soviet Union Republic, recalls its Communist past with a band of red at the top of the tricolor. In the center is a wider band of white, which represents cotton production, the most important part of Tajikistan's economy. The lower band of green is said to stand for the country's other agricultural produce. In the central white band is a gold crown, representing Tajikistan's sovereignty, under an arc of gold stars symbolizing friendship. Tajikistan was one of the last republics to adopt a new flag in 1992, after the collapse of the USSR.

Turkmenistan

Capital city *Ashgabat*
Population *5,171,943*
Land area (sq. mi) *188,455;* **(sq. km)** *488,100*
Currency *1 Turkmen manta = 100 tenge*
Languages *Turkmen, Russian, Uzbek*

Ratio 2:3

A "gul" is a design used in the production of rugs. The national flag of Turkmenistan displays five guls to the hoist side of the flag, which represent the five main tribes that make up the nation. The rest of the flag is dark green, with a white crescent moon and stars depicted in the upper part. Both the colors and the symbols are wellknown in the tradition of Islam. At the foot of the gul design are two crossed olive branches, the UN symbol for peace.

Bhutan

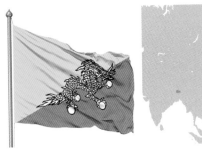

Capital city *Thimphu*
Population *733,643*
Land area (sq. mi) *14,823;* **(sq. km)** *38,394*
Currency *1 ngultrum = 100 chetrum*
Languages *Sharchhopka, Dzongkha, Lhotshamkha*

Ratio 2:3

"Druk Yul" or "The Land of the Thunder Dragon" is the name the people of Bhutan often use for their country. The design of the national flag refers to the nation's Buddhist history, which dates back to the thirteenth century when a monastery called the Druk was set up there. Behind the dragon are two colors, divided diagonally; the lower orange part represents the authority of the Buddhist faith, while the upper yellow part stands for the secular realm. The dragon itself is white, which denotes purity. In its claws, it holds jewels to symbolize the wealth of the country.

Uzbekistan

Capital city *Tashkent*
Population *28,929,716*
Land area (sq. mi) *172,741;* **(sq. km)** *447,400*
Currency *1 Uzbek soum = 100 tiyn*
Languages *Uzbek, Russian, Tajik*

Ratio 1:2

Uzbekistan was the first republic of Central Asia to adopt a new national flag in 1991, after breaking away from the USSR and declaring its sovereignty as an independent state. The flag is made up of equal bands of blue, white, and green; the central band is fimbriated (edged) with red. In the blue band, on the upper hoist side, the familiar Muslim symbols of a white crescent moon and stars are displayed, in this case to symbolize the rebirth of the nation. The twelve stars in this design are said to stand for the twelve signs of the Zodiac.

Nepal

Capital city *Kathmandu*

Population *30,986,975*

Land area (sq. mi) *56,826;* **(sq. km)** *147,181*

Currency *1 Nepalese rupee = 100 paisa*

Languages *Nepali, Maithali, English*

Ratio 4:3

The flag of Nepal is unique in that it is not rectangular, like every other national flag, but has the shape of two overlapping triangles. The shape is based on two pennants that once belonged to rival branches of the Rana dynasty, at one time rulers of Nepal. The upper triangle is smaller than the lower, and shows a stylized crescent moon, lying horizontally. This represents royal authority. The lower triangle displays a white sun, which is a symbol of political power. Together, the two pennants express the hope that Nepal's independence will last as long as the sun and the moon. The red ground of the flag stands for energy, while the blue border denotes peace. The flag was formally adopted in 1962, when the Nepalese constitution was established.

India

Capital city *New Delhi*

Population *1,236,344,631*

Land area (sq. mi) *1,269,213;* **(sq. km)** *3,287,263*

Currency *1 Indian rupee = 100 paise*

Main languages *Hindi, English, Bengali, Telugu, Marathi, Tamil, Urdu, Gujarati, Malayalam*

Ratio 2:3

The national flag of India boasts a distinctive central motif, a blue wheel or "chakra." Known as the "wheel of law," this is the symbol of the first Buddhist emperor, Ashoka, and dates from the third century B.C. It was adopted in 1947 when India gained independence, to give a flavor of the country's history. The design replaced that of Mahatma Gandhi's spinning wheel, which was a symbol of the country's economic self-sufficiency. The colors of the flag are also significant. The orange or saffron band at the top of the tricolor stands for the Hindu faith, while the green band at the bottom denotes Islam. The white band in the middle expresses the hope that the country, and these two faiths, can live in peace and unity.

Bangladesh

Capital city *Dhaka*

Population *166,280,712*

Land area (sq. mi) *55,597;* **(sq. km)** *143,998*

Currency *1 taka = 100 paisa*

Languages *Bangla, English*

Ratio 3:5

A single red circle on a green field gives Bangladesh's national flag a simple yet distinctive design. When the flag was first adopted following independence in 1971, the circle displayed a map of the country in gold or yellow, but this was dropped within a few months, perhaps because it served as a reminder of the partitioning of India and Pakistan. The red disk is said to stand for the dawn of independence and the blood shed in the struggle for freedom, while the green field symbolizes the country's lush landscape. Green is also traditionally the color of Islam. When the flag is flying, the red disk appears to be central, but it is in fact set slightly toward the hoist side so as to achieve this effect.

Sri Lanka

Capital city *Colombo*

Population *21,866,445*

Land area (sq. mi) *25,332;* **(sq. km)** *65,610*

Currency *1 Sri Lankan rupee = 100 cents*

Languages *Sinhala, Tamil*

Ratio 1:2

The "Lion Flag" of Sri Lanka dates back to the ancient Sinhalese kingdom of Kandy, and has for centuries been used as a symbol of justice. It shows a yellow lion on a red field, holding a sword in its front paw. Before 1815, when the country became a British colony, this design was used as the national flag. Later, green and orange bands were added to represent the minority Muslim and Tamil communities. The flag was changed again in 1972, when the country adopted the local name of Sri Lanka in preference to Ceylon. Four leaves were added to the main section, one in each corner of the red field. The four leaves stand for the Buddhist values of metta (compassion), karuna (kindness), muditha (joy), and upeksha (balance).

Maldives

Capital city *Male*
Population *393,595*
Land area (sq. mi) *115;* **(sq. km)** *298*
Currency *1 rufiyaa = 100 laari*
Languages *Maldivian Dhivehi, English*

Ratio 2:3

The Maldives, known locally as "The Thousand Islands," are a group of islands in the Indian Ocean. For many years, their flag was a plain red one. The islands became a British protectorate in the nineteenth century, and achieved independence in 1965. Today, their flag shows a white crescent moon in a green rectangle, set within a red field. The crescent moon is a symbol of Islam, while the green represents the palm trees of the islands, which are an important resource for its people. The red is said to represent the blood of the nation's heroes sacrificed for independence.

British Indian Ocean Territory

Capital city *Diego Garcia*
Population *0*
Land area (sq. mi) *21,003;* **(sq. km)** *54,400*
Currency *1 pound = 100 pence*
Languages *English*

Ratio 1:2

The territory is a group of islands in the Indian Ocean known as the Chagos Archipelago. Formerly, there were other islands in the group, but these were passed to the Seychelles in 1976. Today, the Chagos Islands, the largest of which is Diego Garcia, are a British dependency with an important U.S. military base. The territory's flag features the Union Jack on the upper hoist side, set in a ground of blue wavy lines, to indicate the sea. The palm tree on the fly side represents the islands themselves, while the crown emphasizes their status as a British dependency.

Thailand

Capital city *Bangkok*

Population *67,741,401*

Land area (sq. mi) *198,115;* **(sq. km)** *513,120*

Currency *1 baht = 100 stang*

Languages *Thai, Burmese, English*

Ratio 2:3

Thailand has a national flag known as the Trairanga or tricolor. From ancient times, the country was known as the Kingdom of Siam. In the seventeenth century, the flag was a plain red banner; later, a white elephant was placed at the center. In 1916, a flag showing red and white bands was adopted, and the following year a central blue band was added, to show solidarity with the Allies during World War I. Today, the blue band is said to stand for the monarchy, while the white bands signifies the purity of Buddhism, the national religion of Thailand. The red bands apparently represents the lifeblood of the people. The country's name was changed from Siam to Thailand in 1939, but no change appeared on the national flag.

Myanmar

Capital city *Rangoon*
Population *51,419,420*
Land area (sq. mi) *261,227;* **(sq. km)** *676,578*
Currency *1 kyat = 100 pya*
Language *Burmese*
Ratio 2:3

 The flag of Myanmar, formerly known as Burma, was adopted in 2010. It features a five-pointed white star against three horizontal bands. This background derives from the original tricolor design which followed independence in 1943: the green part of the flag stands for peace, the yellow solidarity, and the red for valor. The white star, once a symbol of the Burmese Resistance during World War II, now denotes the union of the country's five ethnic groups: Burman, Karen, Shan, Kachin, and Chin. Although the country's name was changed in 1989, plans to instate the present flag only emerged following constitutional reforms in 2008.

Singapore

The bicolor flag of Singapore, adopted in 1959, shows a red band at the top and a white one at the bottom. On the top band is a crescent moon and a circle of five stars representing democracy, peace, progress, justice, and equality. The crescent moon and stars are a traditional symbol of Islam, and are thought to have been added to the flag to placate the Muslim Malay minority of Singapore. The official explanation for the design is that it symbolizes the birth of a new nation. Red is said to stand for equality, while white is for purity.

Capital city *Singapore*

Population *5,567,301*

Land area (sq. mi) *269;* **(sq. km)** *697*

Currency *1 Singapore dollar = 100 cents*

Languages *Mandarin, English, Malay, Hokkien*

Ratio 2:3

Malaysia

Capital city *Kuala Lumpur*

Population *30,073,353*

Land area (sq. mi) *127,354;* **(sq. km)** *329,847*

Currency *1 Ringgit = 100 sen*

Languages *Bahasa Malaysia, English, Chinese, Tamil, Teluga, Malayalam, Panjabi, Thai*

Ratio 1:2

The official name for the national flag of Malaysia was chosen in 1997, on the fortieth anniversary of the country's independence. It is "Jalur Gemilang" or "Glorious Stripes." The flag is similar to that of the United States, with a main body of red and white stripes and a dark blue canton on the hoist side. Red and white are traditional colors of the Malagasy people of Southeast Asia, and were later used by European and U.S. ships in the area. The fourteen stripes represent the original member states of the Malaysian Federation. In the blue canton is a yellow crescent moon and a star, also with fourteen points. Yellow is the color of the Sultan of Malaysia, and the crescent moon and star are wellknown symbols of the Islamic faith.

Cambodia

Capital city *Phnom Penh*
Population *15,458,332*
Land area (sq. mi) *69,897;* **(sq. km)** *181,035*
Currency *1 riel = 100 sen*
Languages *Khmer, French, English*

Ratio 2:3

The central emblem of the Cambodian flag is a representation of the twelfth-century temple of Angkor Wat, one of the country's most famous monuments and an ancient symbol of the Khmer monarchy. The towers on the temple are said to represent the peaks of Mount Meru, legendary home of the Hindu gods. Behind the emblem is a wide central band of red, with two narrower bands of blue at top and bottom. The blue represents royalty, the red symbolizes the nation, and the white, religion. This flag was first adopted in 1948, but was dropped in 1970, when the Khmer Republic came into being. When the monarchy was restored in 1993, after a long and bloody civil war, the old flag was reintroduced by Sihanouk, the new king.

Vietnam

Capital city *Hanoi*
Population *93,421,835*
Land area (sq. mi) *127,880;* **(sq. km)** *331,210*
Currency *1 dong = 100 xu*
Languages *Vietnamese, English*
Ratio 2:3

The Vietnamese flag has a striking design of a yellow star, set in the center on a red ground. The design, featuring the color red and the star, makes obvious reference to Vietnam's Communist past. The five points on the star are said to represent the five groups who helped to build socialism in Vietnam: farmers, workers, intellectuals, youths, and soldiers. The single star symbolizes unity in the country, an especially important concept given Vietnam's long history of war, disruption, and control by foreign powers. From the 1950s to the 1970s, Vietnam was divided into North Vietnam, which was closely allied with the USSR and China, and South Vietnam, which was mainly supported by the U.S. In 1975, the Vietnam war ended, and the two republics became a single nation once more.

Laos

Capital city *Vientiane*
Population *6,803,699*
Land area (sq. mi) *91,428;* **(sq. km)** *236,800*
Currency *1 kip = 100 at*
Languages *Lao, French, English*

Ratio 2:3

 The flag of Laos is one of the few Communist flags not to feature a star. Instead, a large white disk is set in a wide blue central band, with narrower red bands at the top and bottom. The blue band stands for the Mekong River that flows through Laos, and the red bands signify the blood shed by the people in defense of their country. The white disk represents the moon over the Mekong River, and is also a symbol of the people's unity. The flag was adopted in 1975, when the Communist Pathet Lao replaced the 600-year-old monarchy.

Brunei

Capital city *Bandar Seri Begawan*
Population *422,675*
Land area (sq. mi) *2,225;* **(sq. km)** *5,765*
Currency *1 Bruneian dollar = 100 sen*
Languages *Malay, English, Chinese*

Ratio 1:2

 The flag of Brueni features a red emblem on a yellow field, with two black and white diagonal stripes running across it. Yellow is the traditional color of the Sultan of Brunei. The black and white stripes were added in 1906 to mark the fact that Brunei had become a British dependency. In 1959, the state arms were added, which show a parasol, a crescent, wings, and hands. The parasol is a symbol of royalty; the crescent denotes Islam; the wings, with four feathers, signify the protection of justice, tranquillity, prosperity, and peace; and the hands are upraised to God.

Indonesia

Capital city *Jakarta*

Population *253,609,643*

Land area (sq. mi) *735,347;* **(sq. km)** *1,904,549*

Currency *1 Indonesian rupiah = 100 sen*

Languages *Bahasa Indonesia, English, Dutch*

Ratio 2:3

The Indonesian flag is known as "Sang Saka Merah Putih" meaning "Lofty Bicolor of Red and White." It dates back to that of the Javanese Majapahit Empire, which dominated Indonesia from the thirteenth to the sixteenth century; it was revived again during the 1920s, when Indonesian nationalists agitated against Dutch rule. (For many years, the Dutch had controlled Indonesia through the Dutch East India Company.) The current flag was adopted in 1945, when the country declared its independence. Red and white are sacred colors in Indonesia: red represents the physical world, and white the spiritual. Red also stands for bravery and freedom, while white also means purity and justice. Another interpretation is that the red stands for palm sugar (red in color), and the white for rice, both staples of Indonesian cuisine.

Timor-Leste

Capital city *Dili*
Population *1,201,542*
Land area (sq. mi) *5,742;* **(sq. km)** *14,874*
Currency *1 U.S. dollar = 100 cents*
Languages *Tetum, Portuguese, Indonesian, English*
Ratio 1:2

Timor-Leste was formerly East Timor, the eastern part of the island of Timor. Until 1975, it was owned by the Portuguese, but in 1975 declared its independence, raising the present flag as its banner. However, Indonesia invaded and occupied the new republic almost immediately. After years of conflict, with the loss of thousands of lives, Timor-Leste once more became independent in 2002, and the flag returned. The flag is based on that of the main political party, Fretilin. The ground of it is red, symbolizing the blood of those who died fighting for freedom. The black triangle stands for the country's dark colonial past, and the yellow arrow for the republic's bright future. Set within this is a white, five-pointed star, the guiding light of peace and freedom.

Philippines

Capital city *Manila*

Population *107,668,231*

Land area (sq. mi) *115,830;* **(sq. km)** *300,000*

Currency *1 Philippine peso = 100 centavos*

Languages *Filipino, English*

Ratio 1:2

The flag of the Philippines was designed by General Emilio Aguinaldo, leader of the Filipino rebellion against the Spanish rulers of the islands at that time. The general defeated the Spanish at the Battle of Alapan on May 28, 1898, a date still celebrated as Flag Day in the Philippines. The red, white, and blue of the flag is thought refer to the U.S., which then took over the islands, promising independence. The symbols on the white triangle are an eight-rayed sun and three stars, representing the dawning of a new era of freedom and self-determination. The eight rays represent the eight provinces that were the first to rise up against the Spanish, while the three stars stand for Mindanao, Luzon, and Visayas, the three main regions of the country.

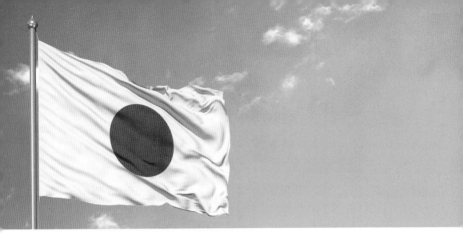

Japan

Capital city *Tokyo*
Population *127,103,388*
Land area (sq. mi) *145,913;* **(sq. km)** *377,915*
Currency *1 Yen = 100 sen (no longer used)*
Language *Japanese*

Ratio 2:3

The Japanese symbol of the red circle on a white ground has been used for more than a thousand years. Known as the "Hinomaru" or "Sun Circle," the design is a simple yet striking illustration of the ancient name for Japan, the "Land of the Rising Sun." Legend has it that the Sun Goddess Amaterasu gave birth to Japan's first emperor, Jimmu, in the seventh century b.c. In the twelfth century a.d., samurai warriors or "bushi" drew sun circles on folding fans called "gunsen." Later, in the fifteenth and sixteenth centuries, sun circles became popular as military insignia and were painted on banners to be used in battle. In 1870, this ancient symbol was officially adopted as the Japanese flag, when Japan began to make links with other countries after many years of isolation.

China

Capital city *Beijing*

Population *1,355,692,576*

Land area (sq. mi) *3,705,389;* **(sq. km)** *9,596,960*

Currency *1 Yuan = 100 fen*

Languages *Mandarin, Yue (Cantonese), Wu (Shanghaiese), Minbei, Minnan, Xiang, Gan, Hakka*

Ratio 2:3

The flag of China was adopted officially in 1949 when Communist leader Mao Zedong founded the People's Republic. The main color of the flag is red, which is both the traditional color of China and the color of revolution and Communism. On the upper hoist side is a design of five yellow stars, one large and the others smaller. The large star is said to represent the Communist Party of China and the smaller ones the four main social classes of the Chinese people: workers, peasants, bourgeoisie, and capitalists. Another explanation is that the large star denotes the Communist Party and the four smaller ones the four other political parties allowed by the state. It is also argued that the five stars represent the main ethnic groups of the country.

Hong Kong

Capital city *Hong Kong*

Population *7,112,688*

Land area (sq. mi) *426;* **(sq. km)** *1,104*

Currency *1 Hong Kong dollar = 100 cents*

Languages *Chinese (Cantonese), English*

Ratio 2:3

The flag of Hong Kong used to be a British blue ensign featuring the emblem of the colony, which dated from 1959. In 1997, China reclaimed Hong Kong, and it is now designated as a Special Administrative Region of China. A local design was rejected by the Chinese government in favor of its own design. The new flag is red, which links it to China's Communist regime. In the center of it is a white bauhinia, or Hong Kong orchid tree, which grows in the region. The flower has five small red stars within the petals, also recalling China's flag.

Macau

Capital city *Macau*

Population *587,914*

Land area (sq. mi) *9;* **(sq. km)** *28*

Currency *1 pataca = 100 avos*

Languages *Portuguese, Chinese (Cantonese)*

Ratio 2:3

The flag of Macau features a stylized motif of a lotus flower with three petals, symbolizing its three islands: the Macau Peninsula, Taipa, and Colôane. Shining over the lotus flower are five stars, which refer the territory's recent change of status to a Special Administrative Region within the People's Republic of China. Also depicted is a bridge, set against a light green ground, which recalls the seawater surrounding the islands. The flag was designed by Xiao Hong, a professor of arts and crafts at Henan University, and adopted in 1999, when Macau passed from the Portuguese to the Chinese.

Mongolia

Capital city *Ulaanbaatar*

Population *2,953,190*

Land area (sq. mi) *603,905;* **(sq. km)** *1,564,116*

Currency *1 togrog = 100 mongos*

Languages *Khalkha Mongol, Turkic, Russian*

Ratio 1:2

The Mongolian flag has a central band of blue, a traditional color of the Mongolian people. On either side are bands of red, and on the hoist side is the national emblem of Mongolia, the "soyombo." This is an ancient Buddhist symbol and it has several interrelated meanings. The fire symbol at the top, with its three tongues of flame, represents past, present, and future; it also signifies the family hearth and the continuity of the people. Further down is the yin and yang symbol, which in Mongolian culture is visualized as two fish, whose ever-open eyes stand for reason and wisdom. On either side of the soyombo are two rectangles, which stand for stone walls. They illustrate a Mongolian proverb, "The friendship of two men is stronger than stone walls."

South Korea

Capital city *Seoul*

Population *49,039,986*

Land area (sq. mi) *38,501;* **(sq. km)** *99,720*

Currency *1 South Korean won = 100 chon*

Languages *Korean, English*

Ratio 2:3

The South Korean flag, called the Taegukki, was adopted in 1950, after the country separated from North Korea. It dates back to a nineteenth-century flag, with a central image of the yin-yang symbol in red and blue set against a white ground. Flanking the symbol on four sides are black trigrams, known as Kwae, which are drawn from the I Ching, the Chinese book of divination and philosophy. The yin-yan symbol expresses harmony through duality and balance, while the four black symbols represent heaven, fire, water, and earth. The white ground stands both for purity and the hope for peace.

North Korea

Capital city *Pyongyang*
Population *24,851,627*
Land area (sq. mi) *46,540;* **(sq. km)** *120,540*
Currency *1 North Korean won = 100 chon*
Language *Korean xu*

Ratio 1:2

The star on the flag of North Korea signals that it is a Communist state. In 1948, when the USSR withdrew, North Korea remained Communist and adopted the present flag. The design shows a wide central band in red, with two narrower bands at the top and the bottom; running between the blue and red bands, on either side, are two narrow white bands. The red stands for the blood of the people shed for the socialist revolution; the blue is for peace; and the white is for purity. The star is also said to represent the "Great Leader" of the country.

Taiwan

Capital city *Taipei*
Population *23,359,928*
Land area (sq. mi) *13,891;* **(sq. km)** *35,980*
Currency *1 new Taiwan dollar = 100 cents*
Languages *Mandarin, Taiwanese, Hakka*

Ratio 2:3

The national flag of Taiwan derives from the flag of the Kuomintang, the Chinese nationalists defeated by the Communists in 1949. The Kuomintang then set up an exile government in Taiwan. The flag is red, a traditional Chinese color, with a blue canton on the upper hoist side. Set in the canton is a white sun with 12 rays, representing the 12 hours of the day and the 12 hours of the night (meaning that the progress of the country is unceasing). The red, white, and blue colors of the flag are said to stand for the "Three Principles of the People:" those of nationalism, democracy, and purity.

AFRICA

The Pan-African tricolor of red, gold, and green appears on many flags of the African continent. The colors were derived from the flag of Ethiopia, which became a beacon of hope for Africa during the nineteenth century as the one country to resist European colonization. For this reason, on achieving independence in the 1960s, many African nations chose the Ethiopian colors for their national flags. The crescent moon and star also appear on many of Africa's national flags, indicating the predominantly Muslim faith of its people in these countries. Some countries, particularly in the south, have used indigenous symbols and emblems on their national flags. For example, the flag of Swaziland features a traditional spear and shield. Finally, there are African countries, such as Rwanda, which have recently redesigned their national flags in an attempt to make a new start after a painful era of warfare and bloodshed.

Egypt

Capital city *Cairo*
Population *86,895,099*
Land area (sq. mi) *386,660;* **(sq. km)** *1,001,450*
Currency *1 Egyptian pound = 100 piastres*
Language *Arabic*
Ratio 2:3

The central motif on the Egyptian national flag is the eagle of Saladin. Saladin was a twelfth-century sultan who recaptured Jerusalem from the crusaders and became a legendary national hero among Arab peoples. Thus the eagle is a powerful symbol of Arab identity and independence. The eagle has a shield on its breast showing the national colors, and stands on a tablet with the name of the country inscribed on it in Arabic characters. It is set in the center of a horizontal tricolor, showing the colors red, white, and black in equal bands across it. The red recalls the period of struggle before the revolution of 1952; the white, the abolition of the monarchy at that time; and the black, the period of monarchical rule and British colonialism.

Sudan

Capital city *Khartoum*

Population *36,108,853*

Land area (sq. mi) *718,719;* **(sq. km)** *1,861,484*

Currency *1 Sudanese pound = 100 piastres*

Languages *Arabic, English, Nubian*

Ratio 1:2

The name "Sudan" is Arabic for black, a reference to the peoples who live in this vast area of northern Africa. For many years, since independence in 1956, the country has been troubled by civil war and famines. The flag displays the Pan-Arab colors: red, white, and black bands are intersected by a green triangle on the hoist side. According to the Sudanese government, the flag's colors represent the following: red stands for struggle, the martyrs of the Sudan, and the Great Arab Land; white stands for Islam, peace, optimism, light, and love; black stands for Sudan and the Mahdiya revolution; and, finally, green stands for prosperity and agriculture.

South Sudan

Capital city *Juba*
Population *12,042,910*
Land area (sq. mi) *248,777;* **(sq. km)** *644,329*
Currency *1 South Sudanese pound = 100 piastres*
Languages *English, Arabic, regional languages*
Ratio 1:2

During the struggle with the north of Sudan in the 1990s, the Sudan People's Liberation Army created a banner of independence, which was raised for the first time as South Sudan's national flag when the country gained independence in July 2011. Bearing a striking resemblance to the flags of Sudan and neighbouring Kenya, both in proportion and the use of Pan-African colors, the addition of blue represents the waters of the River Nile which provide sustenance for the land, while the white represents the peace attained following Africa's longest running conflict. The yellow five-pointed star represents the unity of the states in South Sudan.

Libya

Capital city *Tripoli*
Population *6,244,174*
Land area (sq. mi) *679,359;* **(sq. km)** *1,759,540*
Currency *1 Libyan dinar = 1,000 dirhams*
Languages *Arabic, Italian, English*
Ratio 1:2

The present Libyan flag is identical to the one adopted when the country achieved independence in 1951. At its center is a white crescent moon and a star—symbols of Islam. The wide black field recalls the banner of the Senussi dynasty of Cyrenaica to which Idris, the first and only king of Libya, belonged. The upper red band represents the region of Fezzan and the green Tripolitania. The flag was in use until Colonel Gaddafi seized power in 1969. For most of the Gaddafi era, Libya's flag was plain green—the only national flag in the world to feature no design or insignia of any sort. The 1951 flag was officially re-adopted by the country's National Transitional Council in 2011, after Gaddafi's fall.

Tunisia

Capital city *Tunis*
Population *10,937,521*
Land area (sq. mi) *63,169;* **(sq. km)** *163,610*
Currency *1 Tunisian dinar = 1,000 millimes*
Languages *Arabic, French, Berber*

Ratio 2:3

The Tunisian national flag echoes that of Turkey, which ruled the country for centuries. The flag was first adopted in 1835 to show that Tunisia was part of the Ottoman Empire. Like the Turkish flag, the Tunisian flag shows a crescent moon and a star as its central design. These are well-known symbols of the Islamic faith. However, on the Tunisian flag the colors are reversed out, so that the moon and star are red. The symbols are set on a white disk, which is said to represent the sun. This version of the flag, with some small adaptations, has survived from the nineteenth century, throughout a long period of French rule from 1881 to 1956, to the present day. When Tunisia achieved independence in 1956, the flag was retained.

Algeria

Capital city *Algiers*

Population *38,813,722*

Land area (sq. mi) *919,589;* **(sq. km)** *2,381,740*

Currency *1 Algerian dinar = 100 centimes*

Languages *Arabic, French, Berber dialects*

Ratio 2:3

The bicolor national flag of Algeria is green and white, with a central symbol of a crescent moon and star in red. The green section of the flag stands for Islam; the white is associated with purity. White also recalls the national hero Abd al-Kadir, who led the resistance to the French during the nineteenth century, adopting a white flag as his standard. The crescent moon and star are emblems of Islam; their red color here stands for the blood of national heroes spilled in the struggle for independence. The flag is based on a design created in 1928 for the Algerian National Liberation Front, and was used as the flag of the government in exile from 1958 to 1962. It was officially adopted in 1962 when Algeria achieved independence from France.

Morocco

Capital city *Rabat*

Population *32,987,206*

Land area (sq. mi) *172,413;* **(sq. km)** *446,550*

Currency *1 Moroccan dirham = 100 centimes*

Languages *Arabic, Berber dialects, French*

Ratio 2:3

The green five-pointed star in the center of the Moroccan national flag is known as the "Seal of Solomon." This ancient symbol, which dates back thousands of years, was added to the flag in 1915, to distinguish the country's plain red banner from those of other Arab nations. Since the sixteenth century, Red has been the traditional color of the Moroccan flag. In Morocco, the color is said to signify the blood ties between the Prophet Mohammed and the King, who bears the title of Commander of the Believers. During the period of French colonization, Morocco retained the red flag. As with other North African colonies, the French tricolor of red, white, and blue was not used. In 1956, when Morocco became independent from France, the red flag was retained.

Mauritania

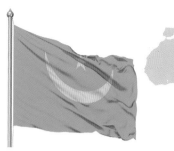

Capital city *Nouakchott*
Population *3,516,806*
Land area (sq. mi) *397,953;* **(sq. km)** *1,030,700*
Currency *1 ouguiya = 5 khoums*
Languages *Arabic, Pulaar, Soninke, Wolof, French*
Ratio 2:3

The colors and symbols of the Mauritanian national flag mark it both as an African and as an Islamic nation. Green and yellow are two of the Pan-African colors, and are also used in Islam, while the crescent moon and star are traditional symbols of the Islamic faith. Under the Almoravid dynasty in the eleventh and twelfth centuries, the country became an important center for Islam, and its people helped to spread the Muslim faith throughout North Africa. The current flag was adopted in 1959, a year before the nation became independent from French rule which began in the twentieth century.

The Gambia

Capital city *Banjul*
Population *1,925,527*
Land area (sq. mi) *4,362;* **(sq. km)** *11,295*
Currency *1 dalasi = 100 bututs*
Languages *English, Mandinka, Wolof, Fula*
Ratio 2:3

The Gambia gained independence from Britain in 1965, when it adopted its present-day flag. The flag features a horizontal blue band running through the center, flanked by two narrow white bands on either side. At the top of the flag is a wide red band, and at the bottom, a wide green one. The symbolism of the flag is as follows: the blue band represents the Gambia River running through the country; the red indicates the hot sun shining overhead; and green stands for the land. Another interpretation is that green represents the forests, while red signifies the savannah.

Guinea-Bissau

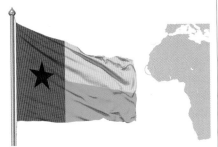

Capital city *Bissau*
Population *1,693,398*
Land area (sq. mi) *13,947;* **(sq. km)** *36,125*
Currency *1 franc = 100 centimes*
Languages *Portuguese, Crioulo*

Ratio 1:2

To celebrate its independence from Portugal in 1973, Guinea-Bissau adopted a new flag showing the Pan-African colors of red, gold, and green, together with a black star, symbol of the African continent. The red runs in a vertical strip on the hoist side, with the other two colors horizontal. The gold band, set above the green, symbolizes the African sun, while the green stands for the fertile land. The flag of Guinea-Bissau is based on that of Ghana, which was the first of the African nations to achieve independence.

Cape Verde

Capital city *Praia*
Population *512,096*
Land area (sq. mi) *1,557;* **(sq. km)** *4,033*
Currency *1 escudo = 100 centavos*
Languages *Portuguese, Crioulo*

Ratio 2:3

The national flag of Cape Verde shows a circle of ten yellow stars, which represent the country's ten islands lying off the coast of Africa. The islands were colonized by the Portuguese in the fifteenth century and later became an important trading center. The circle symbolizes the unity of the Cape Verdean nation, but also refers to the mariner's compass and the helm of a ship. The background color of blue represents the sea and sky, while the red and white stripes running horizontally across the flag symbolize the road to development and progress through the effort of the people.

Senegal

Capital city *Dakar*
Population *13,635,927*
Land area (sq. mi) *75,954;* **(sq. km)** *196,722*
Currency *1 franc = 100 centimes*
Languages *French, Wolof, Pulaar, Jola, Mandinka*
Ratio 2:3

In 1960, Senegal adopted its current national flag, a tricolor whose design is based on that of France. (For many years, France ruled Senegal.) The flag displays the Pan-African colors of green, gold, and red, to show its solidarity and friendship with other African nations. The green is a traditional Muslim color; it is also a symbol of fertility for those who practice Animist religions, of whom there are many in Africa. Gold is said to be the color of art, literature, the intellect, and prosperity. Red stands for the blood of those shed in the struggle for independence. The central star is a common emblem in Africa. The flag replaces a former flag that Senegal shared with Mali, which showed a "kanaga," an African symbol depicting a black man.

Sierra-Leone

Capital city *Freetown*

Population *5,743,725*

Land area (sq. mi) *27,698;* **(sq. km)** *71,740*

Currency *1 leone = 100 cents*

Languages *English, Mende, Temne, Krio*

Ratio 2:3

Sierra Leone's national flag is a horizontal tricolor with equal bands of green (top), white (center), and blue (bottom). The green band is said to represent the lush vegetation of its wooded mountainsides and the agriculture of the nation. The white band, as in many other flags, stands for peace and unity. The blue band symbolizes the waters of the sea around Sierra Leone's coast. The flag was adopted in 1961, when Sierra Leone ceased to be a British colony and became an independent nation. The colors of the flag are thought to derive from Sierra Leone's coat of arms.

Liberia

Capital city *Monrovia*
Population *4,092,310*
Land area (sq. mi) *43,000;* **(sq. km)** *111,370*
Currency *1 Liberian dollar = 100 cents*
Languages *English, ethnic group languages*
Ratio 10:19

The Liberian flag bears witness to its history as a colony for liberated slaves from the United States. Liberia was founded in 1822 by the American Colonization Society to provide a homeland for these slaves. The first flag the colony adopted was similar to the flag used at present, but showed a Christian cross in the blue canton. Later, the cross was replaced by a star to show that Liberia was a single, independent nation. At the time, a local poet said of the star that "after ages of wandering, it has at length found its orbit." The design of the red, white, and blue flag is clearly based on that of the United States. The flag shows eleven stripes, to represent the eleven men who first signed Liberia's declaration of independence.

Cote D'Ivoire

Capital city *Yamoussoukro*

Population *22,848,945*

Land area (sq. mi) *124,501;* **(sq. km)** *322,460*

Currency *1 franc = 100 centimes*

Languages *French, Dioula*

Ratio 2:3

As its name suggests, Cote d'Ivoire was once a French colony, achieving independence in 1960. Like many other African flags, its basic design is modeled on the French tricolor, but displays a different set of colors. The orange band on the hoist side of the flag represents the savannah region of the country; the white band is for the foaming waters of the Sassandra, Bandama, and Komoe rivers; and the green is for the lush tropical rainforests. Other interpretations are that the orange stands for progress; the white represents national unity; and the green signifies hope for the future.

Guinea

Capital city *Conakry*
Population *11,474,383*
Land area (sq. mi) *94,925;* **(sq. km)** *245,857*
Currency *1 Guinean franc = 100 centimes*
Languages *French, ethnic group languages*
Ratio 2:3

The flag of Guinea displays the Pan-African colors of red, gold, and green on a vertical tricolor in the style of the French flag. (Guinea became independent from France in 1958.) The first president of independent Guinea, Sékou Touré, explained the meaning of the colors in a speech. According to him, red evokes the blood of the nation's martyrs and workers; yellow is the color of Guinean gold and of the African sun, source of energy, generosity, and equality to all men; and green is the color of African vegetation. The colors also represent the motto of the nation: Work, Justice, Solidarity.

Mali

Capital city *Bamako*
Population *16,455,903*
Land area (sq. mi) *478,838;* **(sq. km)** *1,240,192*
Currency *1 franc = 100 centimes*
Languages *French, Bambara*

Ratio 2:3

Mali, formerly known as French Sudan, formed the Federation of Mali with Senegal in 1959. The new federation's flag was a tricolor, derived from the French flag, but showing the Pan-African colors of green, yellow, and red. In the center of the federation's flag was a "kanaga," a symbol of a black human figure. Senegal then left the federation, adopting a new flag that replaced the kanaga with a green star in the central yellow band. In 1961, Mali also removed the kanaga from its flag. But instead of replacing it with anything, Mali decided to continue using the plain tricolor. It has been argued that the kanaga was removed to appease the country's Muslims, whose religious beliefs disallowed the representation of the human figure on the country's national flag.

Burkina Faso

Capital city *Ouagadougou*

Population *18,365,123*

Land area (sq. mi) *105,868;* **(sq. km)** *274,200*

Currency *1 franc = 100 centimes*

Languages *French, ethnic group languages*

Ratio 2:3

Burkina Faso was once known as Upper Volta, a former French colony that achieved independence in 1960. During the 1970s and 1980s, the state experienced a series of military coups. In 1984, it was renamed Burkina Faso, meaning "Land of the Incorruptible." In the same year, the nation adopted a new flag. This is a bicolor with equal bands of red (top) and green (bottom), displaying a yellow star as its central symbol. The Pan-African colors (red, green and yellow) reflect the country's unity with other African nations who have achieved independence. The red is said to stand for sacrifice and revolution, while the green represents the fertile land of the country. The yellow star, a well-known symbol of the African continent, signifies the guiding light of the revolution.

Benin

Capital city *Porto-Novo*
Population *10,160,556*
Land area (sq. mi) *43,482;* **(sq. km)** *112,620*
Currency *1 franc = 100 centimes*
Languages *French, Fon, Yoruba*

Ratio 2:3

Benin gained independence from France in 1960, adopting the present flag. This is a green vertical band on the hoist side, with two horizontal bands of yellow (top) and red (bottom). These Pan-African colors emphasize the unity of the African nations that have achieved independence from the colonial regimes of the past. In 1975, the nation, which was then known as the Republic of Dahomey, changed its name to the People's Republic of Benin. To mark the occasion, the flag was also changed, showing a green star against a red field; however, in 1990 the original flag was brought back.

Togo

Capital city *Lome*
Population *7,351,374*
Land area (sq. mi) *21,925;* **(sq. km)** *56,785*
Currency *1 franc = 100 centimes*
Languages *French, Ewe, Mina, Kabye, Dagomba*

Ratio 3:5

The familiar red, green, and yellow colors of the Pan-African movement appear on the national flag of Togo. Also present is the star of Africa, representing the continent. The flag shows a red canton in the upper hoist side, with a white star in the center. Five stripes of green and yellow run across the flag, which are said to signify the five regions of the country: the maritime region, the plateau region, the central region, the Kara region, and the savannah region. The five stripes are also symbols of the five fingers of the hand, and stand for action.

Nigeria

Capital city *Abuja*

Population *177,155,754*

Land area (sq. mi) *356,667;* **(sq. km)** *923,768*

Currency *1 naira = 100 kobo*

Languages *English, Hausa, Yoruba, Igbo, Fulani*

Ratio 1:2

Nigeria adopted its current flag in 1960 to mark the occasion of its independence. Since the nineteenth century, it had been a colony of Britain. The flag was chosen from a competition held in 1959; out of over two thousand entries, the design that was judged the best was this one, by Michael Taiwo Akinkunmi, a student from Ibadan. The original design also showed a red sun, but this was removed. The flag has two vertical strips of green, with a white strip in the center. It is a stylized depiction of the Nigerian landscape, with the Niger River (in white) running through the verdant fields and forests. The white strip also stands for peace and unity, and the green strips denote agriculture—Nigeria's main source of income.

Niger

Capital city *Niamey*
Population *17,466,172*
Land area (sq. mi) *489,188;* **(sq. km)** *1,267,000*
Currency *1 franc = 100 centimes*
Languages *French, Hausa, Djerma*

Ratio 2:3

The three horizontal bands on the national flag of Niger stand for the three main regions of the country. Orange symbolizes the Sahara desert in the north, while green stands for the fertile grassy plains of the south. The white band in the center of the flag signifies the Niger River. In the middle of the white band is an orange disk, which recalls the hot sun of Africa shining down over the river and the land. An alternative interpretation of the colors is that white is for hope, while green is for fraternity. The orange, white, and red colors are also used by Cote D'Ivoire, another African nation colonized by the French. The flag of Niger was adopted in 1959, a year before the country gained independence.

Ghana

Capital city *Accra*
Population *25,758,103*
Land area (sq. mi) *92,097;* **(sq. km)** *238,533*
Currency *1 cedi = 100 pesewas*
Languages *English, African languages*

Ratio 2:3

Ghana was the first African nation to adopt the colors of the Pan-African movement when it achieved independence from Britain in 1957. These were red, gold, and green, the colors of Ethiopia. As the oldest independent African nation, Ethiopia symbolized the movement for liberation among the African nations. The Ghanaian flag shows three horizontal bands of red (top), yellow (center), and green (bottom). On the central band is a single black star. The black star is thought to be taken from the flag of the Black Star Line, a shipping line founded by black activist Marcus Garvey in 1919 to take black people from around the world back to Africa. Red is said to represent the struggle for freedom, gold for the country's mineral wealth, and green its lush forests.

St. Helena

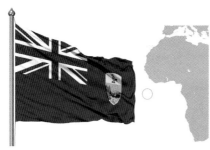

Capital city *Jamestown*
Population *7,415*
Land area (sq. mi) *181;* **(sq. km)** *470*
Currency *1 St. Helena pound = 100 centimes*
Language *English*

Ratio 1:2

The isolated island of St. Helena, famous as Napoleon Bonaparte's place of exile, was once an important port of call for ships from the English East India Company sailing across the southern Atlantic Ocean. However, when the Suez Canal was opened in 1869, it became less important. Today, as a British Crown Colony, its flag shows the British ensign, a blue ground with a Union Jack on the upper hoist side. On the fly side is the island's coat of arms, showing a ship and the rocky shore of the island. Above this is a wirebird, native to the island.

Tristan da Cunha

Capital city *Edinburgh*
Population *297*
Land area (sq. mi) *81;* **(sq. km)** *210*
Currency *1 Tristan pound = 100 pence*
Language *English*

Ratio 1:2

Tristan da Cunha is a remote island in the South Atlantic. It is part of an island group, and along with Gough Island, Inaccessible Island, and the Nightingale Islands, is a dependency of British-owned St. Helena. Accordingly, its flag shows the British ensign of a Union Jack on the upper hoist side, with a blue field. On the fly side of the flag is Tristan da Cunha's coat of arms, which consists of a shield showing four stylized yellow-nosed albatrosses in blue and white. On either side are two spiny lobsters, and underneath is the motto, "Our faith is our strength."

Cameroon

Capital city *Yaounde*

Population *23,130,708*

Land area (sq. mi) *183,567;* **(sq. km)** *475,440*

Currency *1 franc = 100 centimes*

Languages *24 major African language groups,*
English, French

Ratio 2:3

The design of three horizontal stripes on the national flag of Cameroon is based on the French tricolor. However, its colors of red, gold, and green are those of the Pan-African movement. Cameroon was the second modern African state, after Ghana, to adopt these colors on its national flag. In 1961, French Cameroon and British Cameroon, both colonies, joined together in a federation, and two stars were added to the national flag. The country later became one single state, present-day Cameroon, and the two stars were replaced by a single star. Today, the star is said to represent unity; green symbolizes the country's forests; red stands for independence; and yellow is for the savannah regions. Yellow is also said to denote the sun, "the source of the nation's happiness."

Equatorial Guinea

Capital city *Malabo*
Population *722,254*
Land area (sq. mi) *10,830;* **(sq. km)** *28,051*
Currency *1 franc = 100 centimes*
Languages *Spanish, French, pidgin English*

Ratio 2:3

 Equatorial Guinea's national flag has an unusual emblem in the center. This is a gray or silver shield with a silk-cotton tree on it, a species which is native to the island. Over the shield are six gold stars, representing the mainland and the five offshore islands. Underneath the shield is the motto: Unity, Peace, Justice. The coat of arms is set in a central white band, flanked by a green band above and a red band below. Intersecting the bands on the hoist side is a blue triangle, signifying the Pacific Ocean. The flag was adopted in 1979.

Central African Republic

Capital city *Bangui*
Population *5,277,959*
Land area (sq. mi) *240,534;* **(sq. km)** *622,984*
Currency *1 franc = 100 centimes*
Languages *French, Sangho*

Ratio 3:5

 The flag of the Central African Republic has an unusual design with a red vertical band in the center and four horizontal bands running across it. The colors red, white, and blue refer to its history as a former colony of France. The red, yellow, and green Pan-African colors signify its solidarity with other African nations. Linking these is the central red band, which serves as a reminder of the common blood of humanity. On the upper hoist side, set in the top blue band of the flag, is a single yellow star, a symbol of African unity and progress.

Congo

Capital city *Brazzaville*

Population *4,662,446*

Land area (sq. mi) *132,046;* **(sq. km)** *342,000*

Currency *1 franc = 100 centimes*

Languages *French, Lingala and Monokutuba, Kikongo*

Ratio 2:3

In 1958, the former French region of Middle Congo became an autonomous republic with the French Community, and adopted the present-day flag. In 1969, a Communist government came into power and a Soviet-style red flag, with a star and symbols of tools for agriculture and industry, replaced the original one. In 1991, the Communist regime came to an end, and by the following year, a democratically elected government was in power, which restored the original flag. The Congolese flag is divided diagonally from the lower hoist side to the upper fly side by three bands of green, yellow, and red. The central yellow strip is narrower than the ones on each side. The colors are those of the Pan-African movement, which shows solidarity with the other independent nations of Africa.

Gabon

Capital city *Libreville*
Population *1,672,597*
Land area (sq. mi) *103,346;* **(sq. km)** *267,667*
Currency *1 franc = 100 centimes*
Main languages *French, Fang, Myene, Nzebi*

Ratio 3:4

The flag of Gabon shows the nation's political and historic links not only to the Pan-African movement, but also to its former colonizers, the French. The colors green and yellow on the top and middle bands are taken from the flag of Ethiopia, and symbolize African independence (Ethiopia is the oldest independent African nation). The bottom band of blue recalls the French tricolor, as does the three-color design. Additionally, the green stands for the country's rainforests and for its timber trade; the yellow stands for the Equator that runs through the country; and the blue is for the Atlantic Ocean.

São Tomé and Príncipe

Capital city *São Tomé*
Population *190,428*
Land area (sq. mi) *372;* **(sq. km)** *964*
Currency *1 dobra = 100 centimos*
Language *Portuguese, Forro, Cabo Verdian, French*

Ratio 1:2

São Tomé and Príncipe are two islands in the Gulf of Guinea. Formerly Portuguese-owned, the islands achieved independence in 1975, when the national flag was adopted. The design was taken from the banner of the Movimento de Liberacion de São Tomé, which had led the struggle for independence. It features two black stars, representing each of the islands. The colors of the flag come from the Pan-African movement, and show solidarity with other African nations: green is shown on two bands, top and bottom; yellow is on the central band; and red is on a triangle on the hoist side.

Chad

Capital city *N'Djamena*

Population *11,412,107*

Land area (sq. mi) *495,752;* **(sq. km)** *1,284,000*

Currency *1 franc = 100 centimes*

Languages *French, Arabic, Sara*

Ratio 2:3

The Republic of Chad has a national flag that is based on the French tricolor. However, instead of the colors red, white, and blue, the flag uses the colors red, yellow, and blue, with the yellow in the central vertical band. In such a way, two of the colors of France, and two of Africa, are present. In Chad's flag, blue is said to stand for the sky and the waters of the south; yellow signifies the sun and the desert in the north; and red denotes bravery in the struggle for national liberation. The flag was adopted in 1959.

Democratic Republic of the Congo

Capital city *Kinshasa*

Population *77,433,744*

Land area (sq. mi) *905,350;* **(sq. km)** *2,344,858*

Currency *1 Congolese franc = 100 centimes*

Main languages *French, Lingala, Kingwana*

Ratio 3:4

The flag of the Democratic Republic of the Congo was adopted in 2006. Before that, when the country was known as Zaire, the national flag was a light green flag, with a central yellow circle in which a right hand held a torch with a red flame. The present flag represents a return to the design that was first instituted in 1963, three years after independence—except that the blue was changed from royal blue to a lighter sky blue, representing peace. The red stripe represents the blood of those who died for their country, the golden yellow the nation's wealth. The star—a very common motif on national flags—is in this instance a symbol of a radiant future for the nation.

Angola

Capital city *Luanda*
Population *19,088,106*
Land area (sq. mi) *481,351;* **(sq. km)** *1,246,700*
Currency *1 kwanza = 100 lwei*
Languages *Portuguese, Bantu*

Ratio 2:3

The national flag of Angola features a striking design in yellow on a bicolor of red and black. The central motif is a five-pointed star set within half a cogwheel, which is crossed by a machete. This emblem clearly echoes that of the Communist hammer and sickle. The star indicates socialism, while the cogwheel stands for industry. The machete represents the peasants of the agricultural sector. The yellow color of the emblem is said to indicate Angola's mineral resources, while the red of the flag's upper half recalls the blood shed by patriots in the struggle for independence. The black lower half of the flag stands for Africa. The flag was adopted in 1975, and was taken from the banner of the nationalist MPLA (Movimento Popular de Libertação de Angola).

Lesotho

Capital city *Maseru*
Population *1,942,008*
Land area (sq. mi) *11,720;* **(sq. km)** *30,355*
Currency *1 loti = 100 lisente*
Languages *Sesotho, English, Zulu, Xhosa*

Ratio 2:3

The intriguing object at the center of the tricolor flag of Losotho is a conical hat called a mokorotlo. It is part of the traditional dress of the country, and is particularly associated with Moshoeshoe, founder of the nation. The flag was introduced in 2006, on the fortieth anniversary of independence, as a replacement for the flag that had been in use since the coup of 1986. That flag featured a silhouette of a shield, a knobbed club, and a lance. The new flag was explicitly intended to project a peaceful image of the country, and to echo the (white) mokorotlo that was part of the national flag before the coup. The blue band on the flag represents rain water, the white band peace, and the green prosperity.

Namibia

Capital city *Windhoek*

Population *2,198,406*

Land area (sq. mi) *318,259;* **(sq. km)** *824,292*

Currency *1 Namibian dollar = 100 cents*

Languages *Oshiwambo languages, Nama, Afrikaans, English*

Ratio 2:3

Namibia's flag was chosen by a committee in 1990 after a competition to design a new flag for the nation. A blue triangle on the hoist side with a sun recalls the sky, the ocean, and the necessity for rain. The central diagonal red band represents the Namibian people's hope for equality, while the green triangle on the lower fly side stands for the country's agricultural resources. The two narrow white bands on either side of the central red band stand for peace and unity. The colors are drawn from the banner of SWAPO (South West African People's Organization).

South Africa

Capital city *Pretoria*

Population *48,375,645*

Land area (sq. mi) *470,691;* **(sq. km)** *1,219,090*

Currency *1 rand = 100 cents*

Languages *IsiZulu, IsiXhosa, Afrikaans, English, Sepedi, Setswana, Sesotho*

Ratio 2:3

After South Africa's first multi-racial elections in 1994, when the African National Congress (ANC) came to power, a new flag was adopted. Its most striking feature is the horizontal "Y" shape that runs across it, from the hoist side to the fly side. The meaning of this is "convergence:" that South Africa must go forward into the future with its disparate groups united. The many colors of the flag, sometimes called "the rainbow flag," echo this aim, and seek to include all the major political and ethnic groupings of the country. The black, green, and yellow are drawn from the banner of the ANC; the red, white, and blue come from the colors of the former Boer republics; and the colors of the Zulu Inkatha Freedom Party are also present.

Swaziland

Capital city *Mbabane*

Population *1,419,623*

Land area (sq. mi) *6,704;* **(sq. km)** *17,363*

Currency *1 lilangeni = 100 cents*

Languages *English, Siswati*

Ratio 2:3

 Swaziland has a unique national flag that displays a stylized image of the traditional weapons of the Emasotsha warrior. This consists of the warrior's shield, in black and white, and behind it three weapons: a staff and two spears or "assegais." From the weapons hang blue tassels of feathers, which symbolize the royal line of the Swazi people. The shield is set in a dark red central band, symbolizing the blood shed in past struggles, flanked by two yellow bands either side and two blue bands at the top and bottom. The black and white of the shield represents racial harmony.

Botswana

Capital city *Gaborone*

Population *2,155,784*

Land area (sq. mi) *224,606;* **(sq. km)** *581,730*

Currency *1 pula = 100 thebe*

Languages *Setswana, Kalanga, English*

Ratio 2:3

Botswana's national flag is simple but striking. A horizontal black band runs across it, edged on either side by narrow white bands. Above and below the central bands are two wide bands of bright blue. The black and white design is said to be inspired by the zebra, the national animal of Botswana. These colors also represent the country's varied ethnic groups, and the hope that they can live together in racial harmony. The wide blue bands stand for water, a crucial necessity in the arid climate of the country. The flag was adopted when Botswana became independent in 1966.

Zimbabwe

Capital city *Harare*

Population *13,771,721*

Land area (sq. mi) *150,871;* **(sq. km)** *390,757*

Currency *1 Zimbabwean dollar = 100 cents*

Languages *English, Shona, Sindebele*

Ratio 1:2

The colors of the Zimbabwean flag echo those of the ruling African National Union Patriotic Front. The flag was adopted in 1980, when the country gained independence. The flag displays a black stripe running across the center, flanked by red, yellow, and green stripes on either side, and intersected by a white triangle on the hoist side. On the triangle is the image of a bird found carved on soapstone in the ancient city of Zimbabwe. Behind the bird is a star, representing the party's socialist origins. As well as their political meaning, the colors of the flag are said to represent the native people (black), the blood shed in the liberation struggle (red), mineral wealth (yellow), and the fertile land (green). The white of the triangle stands for peace.

Mozambique

Capital city *Maputo*

Population *24,692,144*

Land area (sq. mi) *308,640;* **(sq. km)** *799,380*

Currency *1 metical = 100 centavos*

Languages *Emakhuwa, Portuguese, Xichangana*

Ratio 5:8

The national symbols of Mozambique are depicted on its flag: a rifle, signifying the fight for freedom; a hoe, representing agricultural labor; and a book, which is a reminder of the importance of education. The design of the flag is based on that of the Front for the Liberation of Mozambique (Frelimo), which led the way in the country's struggle for independence. A black band runs horizontally across the center of the flag, the color being a symbol of Africa. On either side are two narrower bands of white, which stands for peace. At the top is a green band, representing the fertile land and at the bottom is a yellow band, indicating mineral wealth. A red triangle on the hoist side shows a yellow star and the national symbols.

Malawi

Capital city *Lilongwe*

Population *17,337,468*

Land area (sq. mi) *45,745;* **(sq. km)** *118,480*

Currency *1 Malawian kwacha = 100 tambala*

Languages *English, Chichewa*

Ratio 2:3

 The flag of the Malawi Congress Party was the inspiration for Malawi's national flag, adopted in 1964 when the country achieved independence. The flag displays three horizontal bands: black at the top, red in the center, and green at the bottom. The black stands for the African people; the red is a tribute to the blood of the people spilled in the struggle for freedom; and the green represents the fertile land. On the black band is the symbol of a red rising sun, which symbolizes the dawn of independence for Malawi. It is also a reminder of the meaning of the name "Malawi," which is "flaming waters," a description of Lake Nyasa at sunset. The symbol of the rising sun also appears on the Malawi coat of arms.

Zambia

Capital city *Lusaka*
Population *14,638,505*
Land area (sq. mi) *290,584;* **(sq. km)** *752,614*
Currency *1 Zambian kwacha = 100 ngwee*
Languages *Bemba, Nyanja, Tonga, Chewa, Lozi, Nsenga, Tumbuka, Lala*

Ratio 2:3

Unusually, the design of Zambia's national flag displays its distinctive markings on the fly rather than on the hoist side of the flag. The main ground of the flag is green, which denotes the country's fertile land. Three bands of color appear on the lower fly side: red, black, and orange. These are taken from the colors of the United Nationalist Independence Party, which led the country's struggle for independence, achieved in 1964. Red also stands for the blood shed in the fight for liberation, while black signifies the African people. Orange indicates the country's copper resources, which are an important part of the Zambian economy. Over the bands of color is an eagle, taken from the country's coat of arms. This is said to symbolize the hope of the people.

Madagascar

Capital city *Antananarivo*

Population *23,201,926*

Land area (sq. mi) *226,656;* **(sq. km)** *587,040*

Currency *1 Malagasy ariary = 100 centimes*

Languages *French, Malagasy*

Ratio 2:3

Madagascar's national flag has a vertical white band on the hoist side, and horizontal bands of red (top) and green (bottom) on the fly side. The island's first inhabitants are thought to have been of Indonesian and African descent. Later, in the eighteenth century, a powerful monarchy arose among the Merina, a people of Malay origin that lived on the central plateau of the island. Their red and white flag became a symbol of Madagascar's attempts to remain independent, as European colonizers began to encroach on the island. Red stands for sovereignty, while white is for purity, and green for hope.

Seychelles

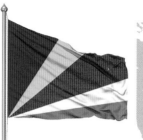

Capital city *Victoria*
Population *91,650*
Land area (sq. mi) *175;* **(sq. km)** *455*
Currency *1 Seychelles rupee = 100 cents*
Languages *Creole, English, French*
Ratio 1:2

 The dramatic flag of the Seychelles features five bands of blue, yellow, red, white, and green, which radiate out from the bottom corner of the hoist side. The design is said to represent a dynamic young country moving into a new future. Blue stands for the sky and sea, and yellow for the sun. Red is the color of the people and white is for harmony. Green, as in many other flags, is for the natural environment. The array of colors is also thought to represent all the colors of the Seychelles' political parties. The flag was adopted in 1996.

Burundi

Capital city *Bujumbura*
Population *10,395,931*
Land area (sq. mi) *10,745;* **(sq. km)** *27,830*
Currency *1 Burundi franc = 100 centimes*
Languages *Kirundi, French, Swahili*
Ratio 3:5

 The white saltire of the Burundi flag has a white disk in the center, on which are three red stars. These illustrate the national motto: "Unity, Work, Progress." They also stand for the three ethnic groups of the country: the Hutu, the Tutsi, and the Twa (a pygmy people). The green sections of the flag, at the house and fly sides, signify hope for the future, while the red sections commemorate those killed fighting for freedom. The white cross denotes peace. The design was adopted in 1967, replacing a previous flag showing monarchist emblems.

Uganda

Capital city *Kampala*
Population *35,918,915*
Land area (sq. mi) *93,064;* **(sq. km)** *241,038*
Currency *1 Ugandan shilling = 100 cents*
Languages *English, Ganda, Luganda, Niger-Congo languages, Nilo-Saharan languages, Swahili, Arabic*
Ratio 2:3

 Black, yellow, and red were the original colors of the Ugandan People's Congress which came to power in 1962. Black is said to stand for the African people, yellow symbolizes the sun, and red represents the brotherhood of races. At the center of the flag is a white disk showing a stylized image of a red-crested crane, the national bird of Uganda. This emblem featured on the country's coat of arms when it was a British colony. The bird stands on one leg and faces the hoist side of the flag, with plumage that reflects that national colors of black, yellow, and red. It symbolizes the progress of Uganda. The national flag has remained unchanged since 1962, despite many turbulent political changes and several military coups over the succeeding years.

Rwanda

Capital city *Kigali*

Population *12,337,138*

Land area (sq. mi) *10,169;* **(sq. km)** *26,338*

Currency *1 Rwandan franc = 100 centimes*

Main languages *Kinyarwanda, French, English*

Ratio 2:3

Rwanda's new national flag was adopted in 2002, in a symbolic gesture to show that the horrifying genocide of the previous decade was over. The flag shows three bands of color: a wide blue top band, a narrower band of yellow (center), and one of green (bottom). A yellow sun shines from the upper fly side on the blue band. The flag was designed by Alphonse Kirimobenecyo, a Rwandan artist and engineer. The blue stands for peace after the violence of the civil war; the yellow represents the hope of rebuilding the economy; and the green is for prosperity.

Kenya

Capital city *Nairobi*

Population *45,010,056*

Land area (sq. mi) *224,079;* **(sq. km)** *580,367*

Currency *1 Kenyan shilling = 100 cents*

Languages *English, Kiswahili*

Ratio 2:3

The imposing shield of a Masai warrior graces the national flag of Kenya. The flag consists of three main horizontal bands of color: black (top), red (center), and green (bottom). The colors are those of the Kenya African National Union Party, which for many years led the struggle for independence from colonial rule. They also symbolize the African people (black), the common blood of humanity (red), and the fertile land of Kenya (green). Two narrow bands of white at each side of the center make reference to a rival political party, the Kenya African Democratic Union Party, and also stand for peace and unity. The Masai shield in the center has two spears crossed behind it, which emphasize the defense of the country's freedom. The flag was adopted in 1963.

Tanzania

Capital city *Dodoma*
Population *49,639,138*
Land area (sq. mi) *365,752;* **(sq. km)** *947,300*
Currency *1 Tanzanian shilling = 100 cents*
Languages *Kiswahili, Kiunguju, English, Arabic*
Ratio 2:3

In 1964, the states of Tanganyika and Zanzibar joined together to become the new republic of Tanzania. To mark the occasion, the flags of both former nations were merged to make a new design. The green, black, and yellow bands of Tanganyika's original flag were retained, and Zanzibar's blue band was added. All the bands were rearranged diagonally instead of horizontally, with the black band in the center, flanked by two narrow bands of yellow, and triangles of green and blue at the top and bottom respectively. In the new design, the green triangle of Tanganyika symbolizes agriculture, the mainstay of the country's economy, while the blue triangle of Zanzibar represents the Indian Ocean. The black central band signifies Tanzania's people, and the yellow bands indicate its mineral resources, especially gold.

Mauritius

Capital city *Port Louis*
Population *1,331,155*
Land area (sq. mi) *787;* **(sq. km)** *2,040*
Currency *1 Mauritian rupee = 100 cents*
Main languages *Creole, Bhojpuri, French, English*
Ratio 2:3

 The flag of Mauritius has four equal horizontal bands, instead of the usual three adopted by many countries. At the top of the flag is a red band, which is said to represent independence. Below that, a blue band symbolizes the Indian Ocean. In the lower half of the flag, a yellow band stands for the island's bright future, while a bottom band of green signifies its lush vegetation. The colors derive from the country's coat of arms, awarded to Mauritius by Kind Edward VII in 1906. The current flag was adopted in 1968, when Mauritius achieved independence from Britain.

Comoros

Capital city *Moroni*
Population *766,865*
Land area (sq. mi) *862;* **(sq. km)** *2,235*
Currency *1 Comoran franc = 100 centimes*
Languages *Arabic, French, Shikomoro*
Ratio 3:5

 Comoros is a group of islands in Southern Africa. At the hoist side, its national flag displays a green triangle with a white crescent and a vertical line of four white stars. These are all familiar symbols of the Islamic faith. On the fly side, there are four bands of color: yellow at the top, white below, red in the lower half of the flag, and blue at the bottom. The four stars and four colored bands represent the four main islands of the group. One of these, Mayotte, is currently administered by France, but sovereignty over it is claimed by Comoros.

Somalia

Capital city *Mogadishu*
Population *10,428,043*
Land area (sq. mi) *246,199;* **(sq. km)** *637,657*
Currency *1 Somali shilling = 100 cents*
Languages *Somali, Arabic, Italian, English*

Ratio 2:3

The blue of the Somali flag derives from that of the UN, which once administered part of the territory. Somalia came into being in 1960 after British Somalia and Italian Somaliland merged together. Italian Somaliland had been a United Nations Trust Territory for the previous decade. In the center of the flag is a white, five-pointed star representing the five areas where Somali people live: northern Somalia, southern Somalia, northern Kenya, southern Ethiopia, and Djibouti. The star is also a symbol of freedom, while white signifies the hope of peace and prosperity. This is an important aspiration for a country that has been the site of civil war, famine, and general turmoil for many years. The flag was first adopted by southern Somalia in 1954.

Ethiopia

Capital city *Addis Ababa*

Population *96,633,458*

Land area (sq. mi) *426,370;* **(sq. km)** *1,104,300*

Currency *1 birr = 100 cents*

Languages *Oromo, Amharic, Somali, Tigrigna, Sidamo, Wolaytta, Gurage*

Ratio 1:2

Ethiopia has been uniquely successful in its resistance to colonial rule, except for a brief period of Italian occupation during World War II. As the oldest independent country in Africa, Ethiopia represents the struggle for liberation against European colonial powers on the African continent. For this reason, the green, yellow, and red colors of its flag were adopted by emerging nations all over Africa, and have become known as the Pan-African colors. The three colors also have an ancient religious significance in Coptic Christianity. They stand for the Holy Trinity and for the Christian values of faith, hope, and charity. The emblem in the center of the tricolor, added in 1996, shows a golden pentangle with four rays, set on a light blue disk, and signifies equality among the Ethiopian people.

Eritrea

Capital city *Asmara*
Population *6,380,803*
Land area (sq. mi) *45,405;* **(sq. km)** *117,600*
Currency *1 nafka = 100 cents*
Main languages *Tigrinya, Arabic, English, Tigre*
Ratio 1:2

The flag of the Eritrean People's Liberation Front is the inspiration for the country's national flag. For many years, the EPLF led Eritrea's struggle for independence from neighboring Ethiopia. Today, the country's national flag recalls this history, with a red triangle symbolizing the blood shed fighting for freedom. The green triangle in the upper fly side stands for agriculture, while the blue one in the lower fly side signifies the sea. In the red triangle is an olive wreath and branch picked out in yellow. This design was adopted in 1995 and replaced the previous symbol of a yellow star.

Djibouti

Capital city *Djibouti*
Population *810,179*
Land area (sq. mi) *8,957;* **(sq. km)** *23,200*
Currency *1 Djiboutian franc = 100 centimes*
Languages *French, Arabic, Somali, Afar*
Ratio 2:3

Djibouti was once known as French Somaliland, and achieved independence from France in 1977, when it adopted its current flag. The flag is based on that of the People's League for Independence, which helped lead the country's struggle for freedom and self-determination. It shows a light blue band at the top, and a green one at the bottom. Light blue is the color of the Somali Issas people, while green is for the Muslim Afars. The bands are intersected by a white triangle, symbolizing peace, on which is a red, five-pointed star, representing the unity of the nation.

OCEANIA

Many of the countries of Oceania show their current or historic links with Britain by displaying the Union Jack on the upper hoist side of their national flags. This is often supplemented with white stars on a blue ground, symbolizing islands or groups of islands in the Pacific Ocean. Typically, the stars are grouped according to the Southern Cross constellation, which is prominent in the night sky of the region. Both these elements—the Union Flag and the Southern Cross—appear on the national flags of Australia and New Zealand. In contrast, some countries have added local symbols and emblems to illustrate their unique culture. For example, the flag of Papua New Guinea displays a yellow bird of paradise as well as the Southern Cross. In recent times, the Aboriginal flag has begun to be recognized and flown in Australia as a mark of respect to the country's indigenous people.

Australia

Capital city *Canberra*

Population *22,507,617*

Land area (sq. mi) *2,988,888;* **(sq. km)** *7,741,220*

Currency *1 Australian dollar = 100 cents*

Languages *English, native languages*

Ratio 1:2

Australia's national flag reflects its historical links with Britain and its geographical position on the globe. It is based on the British Ensign, with a dark blue ground and a Union Flag, also called the Union Jack, on the upper hoist side. Below the Union Jack is a large seven-pointed star; six of the points represent the six states of Australia, while one of them stands for its territories. The fly side of the flag shows the Southern Cross constellation, which is very noticeable in the night sky right across the states and territories of Australia. The Aboriginal peoples of Australia also have their own flag, which consists of black and red stripes and a yellow sun. The colors symbolize the black Aboriginal people, the red earth, and the golden sun.

New Zealand

Capital city *Wellington*

Population *4,401,916*

Land area (sq. mi) *103,362;* **(sq. km)** *267,710*

Currency *1 New Zealand dollar = 100 cents*

Languages *English, Maori*

Ratio 1:2

The flag of New Zealand reflects its history as a colony of Britain. A Union Flag, also called the Union Jack, features in the upper hoist quadrant. On the fly side is a group of four red stars, edged in white, which represent the stars of the Southern Cross constellation in the night sky. This emphasizes New Zealand's location in the South Pacific Ocean. The whole design is set on a royal blue ground, and is based on the British Blue Ensign. According to the New Zealand government, the blue ground also represents the blue sea and clear sky surrounding the country. The flag was originally designed in 1869 to be used at sea, but was adopted as New Zealand's national flag, to be flown on land, in 1902.

Vanuatu

Capital city *Port-Vila*
Population *266,937*
Land area (sq. mi) *4,706;* **(sq. km)** *12,189*
Currency *1 vatu = 100 centimes*
Languages *Bislama, English, French*

Ratio 19:36

This group of Pacific islands, formerly known as the New Hebrides, was jointly administered by France and Britain until 1980. When it achieved independence, it took a new name Vanuatu, and a new flag. The flag features the emblem of a pig's tusk and two crossed namele ferns, both traditional Vanatuan symbols indicating peace and prosperity respectively. The yellow emblem is set on a black triangle at the hoist side, intersecting two bands of red (top) and green (bottom). A yellow "Y" shape, outlined in black, echoes the pattern of the islands as they appear on the map.

Norfolk Island

Capital city *Kingston*
Population *2,210*
Land area (sq. mi) *13;* **(sq. km)** *34*
Currency *1 Australian dollar = 100 cents*
Languages *English, Norfolk*

Ratio 1:2

Norfolk Island is a remote island in the South Pacific Ocean. It was discovered by Captain Cook in 1774 and later became a penal colony of such brutality that it was known as "Hell in the Pacific." In 1856 it was resettled by Pitcairn Islanders, descendants of the H.M.S. *Bounty* mutineers. The islands' abundance of a particular species of pine tree, known as the Norfolk Island Pine, is reflected on its flag. This features three vertical bands of green, white, and green, with a design of the pine tree in the slightly wider central band. The flag was adopted in 1980.

Papua New Guinea

Capital city *Port Moresby*
Population *6,552,730*
Land area (sq. mi) *178,702;* **(sq. km)** *462,840*
Currency *1 kina = 100 toeas*
Language *Tok Pisin, English, Hiri Motu, indigenous languages*

Ratio 3:4

 The striking flag of Papua New Guinea is divided horizontally to form two triangles, the upper one red and the lower one black. At the center of the upper red triangle is a yellow bird of paradise in flight, while the lower black triangle shows the five stars of the Southern Cross constellation. The bird of paradise, which is locally known as "kumul," symbolizes the country's emergence as a nation. The Southern Cross is a prominent constellation in the night sky in this region, and also symbolizes Papua New Guinea's historic links with Australia and with other nations of the South Pacific. The colors black, yellow, and red reflect the colors used for body decoration—a tradition of the people of the island. The current flag was adopted in 1971, four years before Papua New Guinea became independent.

Solomon Islands

Capital city *Honiara*
Population *609,883*
Land area (sq. mi) *11,156;* **(sq. km)** *28,896*
Currency *1 Solomon Islands dollar = 100 cents*
Language *Melanesian pidgin, English, indigenous languages*

Ratio 1:2

The Solomon Islands are a large group of islands in the South Pacific, spread out over a distance of about 900 miles (1,448 km). The islands resisted colonization for centuries, but eventually came under British and German control in the late nineteenth century. By 1900, all the territory was owned by Britain; it was ceded to Australia in 1920. The Solomon Islands finally became fully independent in 1977. Following a national competition the previous year, the current flag was chosen and adopted. It shows a triangle of blue and one of green, divided by a narrow yellow strip. The five stars on the blue triangle represent the archipelago's five administrative districts (which have since increased to eight). Blue is for the sea, green for the land, and yellow for the sunshine.

Tuvalu

Capital city *Funafuti*
Population *11,468*
Land area (sq. mi) *10;* **(sq. km)** *26*
Currency *1 Tuvaluan dollar = 100 cents*
Languages *Tuvaluan, English, Samoan, Kiribati*
Ratio 1:2

 The nine islands of Tuvalu in the South Pacific are represented on its national flag by nine yellow stars. These are arranged on the fly side of the flag, while on the upper hoist side there is a British Union Jack. Instead of the dark blue field of the British Ensign, the Tuvaluan flag features a light blue ground, symbolizing the Pacific Ocean. Formerly known as the Ellice Islands, Tuvalu achieved independence from Britain in 1978. The name "Tuvalu" means "eight islands" in the local language, and refers to the fact that only eight of the islands were originally inhabited.

Wallis and Futuna

Capital city *Mata-Utu*
Population *15,880*
Land area (sq. mi) *54;* **(sq. km)** *142*
Currency *1 franc = 100 centimes*
Languages *Wallisian, Futunian, French*
Ratio 2:3

 The South Pacific islands of Wallis and Futuna were discovered by the Dutch and the British in the seventeenth and eighteenth centuries. In 1842, France declared the islands a French protectorate. More than a hundred years later, the islanders voted to become a French overseas territory. There are several variations on the islands' local flag, but this one shows a large white Maltese Cross on a red ground. The French tricolor is displayed on the upper hoist side, edged in white. On official occasions, the French flag is used; at other times, both of the flags are flown together.

Cook Islands

Capital city *Avarua*
Population *21,200*
Land area (sq. mi) *92;* **(sq. km)** *236*
Currency *1 New Zealand dollar = 100 cents*
Languages *English, Maori*

Ratio 1:2

The Cook Islands are named after Captain Cook, who first sighted them in 1770. Later, in the nineteenth century, the islands became a British protectorate. At the beginning of the twentieth century, the administration of the islands passed to New Zealand; and today, the Cook Islands are self-governing in free association with New Zealand. The islands' national flag is based on the British Blue Ensign, and shows a Union Jack on the upper hoist side. On the fly side is a circle of fifteen white, five-pointed stars, which represent the fifteen islands in the group. The flag was adopted in 1979.

French Polynesia

Capital city *Papeete*
Population *280,026*
Land area (sq. mi) *1,608;* **(sq. km)** *4,167*
Currency *1 franc = 100 centimes*
Languages *French, Polynesian*

Ratio 2:3

These islands in the South Pacific were annexed by France during the nineteenth century. (Tahiti is the main island within the group.) Their flag is an unusual one. It shows a stylized design of a ship riding the waves with the yellow rays of the sun behind it. The ship is a pirogue, a type of catamaran, and represents the oceangoing Polynesian people of the region. There are five crosses marked on the ship, which symbolize five rowers. They also signify the five main island groups of the territory: Tahiti, Tuamotou, the Gambier Islands, the Tubuai Islands, and Clipperton Island.

Tonga

Capital city *Nuku'alofa*

Population *110,237*

Land area (sq. mi) *289;* **(sq. km)** *748*

Currency *1 pa'anga = 100 seniti*

Languages *Tongan, English*

Ratio 1:2

Tonga is a group of islands in the South Pacific that was once known as "the Friendly Islands." During the nineteenth century, it became a kingdom with a monarch at its head, and to this day continues to be the only monarchy in the Pacific. At the start of the twentieth century, it became a British protectorate. In 1970, Tonga achieved independence and joined the Commonwealth of Nations. Today, its flag has a red ground and features a red cross on a white rectangle on the upper hoist side. Initially, the flag showed the red cross in the center, but this was thought to be too similar to the Red Cross flag and was changed to the present design. The cross is thought to derive from ancient Christian iconography.

Pitcairn

Capital city *Adamstown*
Population *48*
Land area (sq. mi) *18;* **(sq. km)** *47*
Currency *1 New Zealand dollar = 100 cents*
Languages *English, Pitkern*
Ratio 1:2

The flag of Pitcairn Island displays a Union Jack on the upper hoist side, recalling the island's former status as a British colony. The island was settled in 1790 by mutineers from H.M.S. *Bounty* and their families. During the nineteenth century, it became a British colony. On the fly side of the flag is the island's coat of arms, which symbolizes some aspects of the early settlers' life. At the top is a Pitcairn wheelbarrow of the kind that was used on the island for transporting goods over muddy terrain. At the bottom is an anchor, symbolizing the *Bounty*.

Niue

Capital city *Alofi*
Population *2,156*
Land area (sq. mi) *100;* **(sq. km)** *260*
Currency *1 New Zealand dollar = 100 cents*
Languages *Niuean, English*
Ratio 1:2

Once a British protectorate, today Nieu is a self-governing island in free association with New Zealand. The main ground of its flag is yellow, with a Union Jack in the upper canton of the hoist. On the vertical and horizontal lines of the Union Jack are four five-pointed yellow stars; a larger yellow star on a blue disk stands in the center. The official explanation of the flag is that the yellow represents the warm friendship between Niue and New Zealand; the four small stars symbolize the Southern Cross; and the larger star illustrates the self-governing status of the island.

Samoa

Once a German protectorate, Samoa became a trust territory of New Zealand after World War I. The national flag features a red ground with a group of white stars in a blue canton on the upper hoist side. When the flag was adopted in 1948 it displayed four stars, but the following year this was changed to five. The stars represent the Southern Cross constellation prominent in the night sky of the South Pacific, and is a design favored by many of the countries in the region for their national flags. The red of the Samoan flag stands for the blood shed in the struggle for independence, finally achieved in 1962. Blue represents freedom and unity, while white signifies purity. Red and white are also traditional Samoan colors.

Capital city *Apia*

Population *196,628*

Land area (sq. mi) *1,093;* **(sq. km)** *2,831*

Currency *1 tala = 100 sene*

Languages *Samoan (Polynesian), English*

Ratio 1:2

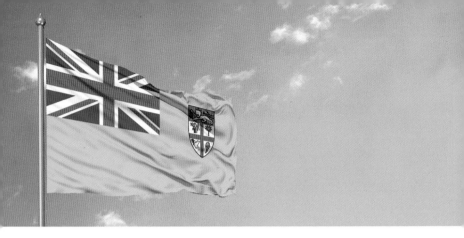

Fiji

Capital city *Suva*

Population *903,207*

Land area (sq. mi) *7,054;* **(sq. km)** *18,274*

Currency *1 Fijian dollar = 100 cents*

Languages *English, Fijian, Hindustani*

Ratio 1:2

Fiji's former status as a colony of Britain is echoed in its national flag, which is based on the Blue Ensign. However, several features mark it out as an independent nation. First, the ground of the flag is light blue, rather than the dark blue of the traditional ensign. (The light blue represents the Pacific Ocean surrounding Fiji.) Second, the Fijian coat of arms appears on the fly side of the flag. This shows a shield with a yellow lion holding a cocoa pod above a cross of St. George. Also displayed are stalks of sugar cane, a coconut palm, a white dove bearing an olive branch, and a bunch of bananas—plants all indigenous to the islands. The flag was adopted in 1970, when Fiji achieved independence.

American Samoa

Guam

Capital city *Pago Pago*

Population *57,902*

Land area (sq. mi) *77;* **(sq. km)** *199*

Currency *1 U.S. dollar = 100 cents*

Languages *Samoan, English*

Ratio 1:2

Capital city *Hagatna*

Population *161,001*

Land area (sq. mi) *210;* **(sq. km)** *544*

Currency *1 U.S. Dollar = 100 cents*

Languages *English, Filipino, Chamorro*

Ratio 22:41

On the national flag of American Samoa, a brown and white bald eagle holds a staff and a war club. The eagle represents the U.S., while the staff and club are Samoan symbols of power and authority. The design of the flag emphasizes the idea that America protects this part of the archipelago, which today is an overseas territory of the U.S. The eagle is displayed on the fly side of the flag, in a white triangle edged in red; two blue triangles complete the design. The colors red, white, and blue are also a reminder of the islands' links with the U.S.

Guam is a strategically important island in the North Pacific Ocean, and today is an overseas territory of the U.S. As such, its national flag is the Stars and Stripes, but the island also has its own territorial flag. This shows a beach scene with a sailboat, a palm tree, and the word "GUAM" in red letters against a bright blue sky. The scene is outlined in red, in an oval teardrop shape, set on a dark blue ground with a narrow red border all around. The territorial flag of Guam is only flown in conjunction with the U.S. flag.

Nauru

Capital city *none*
Population *12,809*
Land area (sq. mi) *8;* **(sq. km)** *21*
Currency *1 Australian dollar = 100 cents*
Languages *Nauruan, English*

Ratio 1:2

Nauru is an island in the Pacific known for its rich phosphate deposits. Its national flag shows a yellow line running across the center, with a star below it, set on the lower hoist side. The ground of the flag is dark blue. The yellow stripe represents the equator, while the star symbolizes Nauru's location in relation to it. The 12 points on the star stand for the 12 original tribes of the island, two of which are now extinct. The flag was adopted in 1968 when Nauru achieved independence. Today, Nauru is the smallest independent republic in the world.

Marshall Islands

Capital city *Majuro*
Population *70,983*
Land area (sq. mi) *70;* **(sq. km)** *181*
Currency *1 U.S. dollar = 100 cents*
Languages *Marshallese, English*

Ratio 10:19

This group of islands in the North Pacific has a national flag with two bands across it, one orange and one white. On the upper hoist side is a star with four large rays, forming a cross, and 20 smaller rays. The star's total of 24 rays represent the 24 districts of the Marshall Islands; the four larger rays stand for its major towns, and also echo the Christian faith of the islanders. The two bands symbolize the chain of islands themselves. The orange and white colors represent hope and wealth, while the deep blue ground denotes the Pacific Ocean.

Kiribati

Northern Mariana Islands

Capital city *Tarawa*
Population *104,488*
Land area (sq. mi) *313;* **(sq. km)** *811*
Currency *1 Australian dollar = 100 cents*
Languages *I-Kiribati, English*
Ratio 1:2

Capital city *Saipan*
Population *78,252*
Land area (sq. mi) *179;* **(sq. km)** *464*
Currency *1 U.S. dollar = 100 cents*
Languages *Philippine languages, Chamorro, English*
Ratio 1:2

Kiribati's national flag was chosen from a competition held in 1979, the year it achieved full independence from Britain. It shows blue and white wavy bands on the lower section of the flag; on the upper section is a yellow sun in the center of a red sky. Over the sun flies a yellow frigate bird. The wavy bands represent the Pacific Ocean, while the frigate bird—a local species—stands for control over the ocean waves. The design is based on the original coat of arms given to the Gilbert and Ellice Islands (now Kiribati and Tuvalu) in 1937.

The Northern Mariana Islands are a group of islands situated in the North Pacific. Their national flag shows a ground of blue, which is derived from the UN flag. (The islands were formerly a trust territory of the UN, administered by the U.S.) In the center of the flag is a large white five-pointed star, set against a stylized image of a "latte" stone. This is a traditional foundation stone used in building and represents the ancient culture of the islands' people. Around the star and stone is a garland of flowers, another symbol of the islanders' traditional culture.

Palau

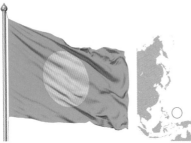

Capital city *Ngerulmud*
Population *21,186*
Land area (sq. mi) *177;* **(sq. km)** *458*
Currency *1 U.S. dollar = 100 cents*
Main languages *Palauan, English, Filipino*
Ratio 5:8

Palau is an island group in the North Pacific, southeast of the Philippines. In 1981, it left the U.S. Trust Territory of the Pacific Islands to become a self-governing republic. At the same time, it adopted its current national flag. The ground of the flag is bright blue, which represents the Pacific Ocean. Just off center, set toward the hoist side of the flag, is a yellow disk. This is said to represent the full moon, and also reflects the islanders' ancient belief that harvesting, fishing, and seed planting are most productive when there is a full moon at night.

Micronesia

Capital city *Palikir*
Population *108,155*
Land area (sq. mi) *271;* **(sq. km)** *702*
Currency *1 U.S. dollar = 100 cents*
Main languages *English, Chuukese, Kosrean*
Ratio 10:19

The Federated States of Micronesia is a group of islands in the North Pacific Ocean. Its national flag has a basic design common to many countries in Oceania: a group of white stars, representing the islands, are set on a blue ground, representing the sea. On the Micronesian flag, the four main islands in the group (Chuuk, Pohnpei, Yap, and Kusrae) are represented by four stars arranged in a diamond pattern. Formerly, from 1962 to 1977, the flag showed six stars, but when the Marshall Islands and the Northern Mariana Islands left the federation, two of the stars were removed.

INTERNATIONAL FLAGS

The essence of international flags is that they should be easily recognizable by, and acceptable to, all peoples across the world, regardless of specific languages, cultures, and religions. Accordingly, international organizations have sought designs that can be understood and accepted by people from many different cultures. In this spirit, the UN flag with its world map, flanked by olive branches on a light blue background, displays the symbols of peace and attempts to avoid political references. The Red Cross has a similar aim: to provide aid to all victims of war and natural disaster, irrespective of their political or religious affiliations. However, the Red Cross has encountered problems, since the cross is historically a Christian symbol. For this reason, the Red Crescent has also been used by aid agencies working in Muslim countries. At present, the movement is considering adopting a nondenominational symbol in keeping with its aim of neutrality.

United Nations

Ratio 2:3

The flag of the United Nations reflects the organization's primary concern to promote world peace. It displays the white emblem of the UN, set in the center of a light blue ground. The emblem is a stylized map of the world showing outlines of all the inhabited continents. The map shows the UN's sphere of influence and is based on a mathematical projection centered on the North Pole. At either side of the map are two golden olive branches, symbolizing peace. The blue and white colors of the flag are also said to signify peace. Today, the blue is often seen on flags of countries who have had close links with the UN, to show their neutrality and independence. The UN emblem was adopted on December 7, 1946.

UNICEF

Ratio 2:3

UNICEF is the United Nations Children's Fund, the arm of the United Nations that works specifically on behalf of children and young people worldwide. Current campaigns focus on emergency aid to children suffering the effects of warfare and natural disasters; medical care, including helping to stop the spread of HIV among children; and provision of education in developing countries. The UNICEF flag emphasizes the organization's aim of protection and care, with a central stylized image of a mother and child in white against a blue field. Also included in the design is part of the UN emblem showing the world map with longitudinal and latitudinal lines.

European Union

Ratio 2:3

The flag of the European Union displays an image of 12 gold stars arranged in a circle at the center of a blue field. The circle is said to represent unity, while the number of stars was chosen as a general number to avoid political references: there are 12 hours on the clock, 12 months in the year, and so on. The flag was initially that of the Parliamentary Assembly of the Council of Europe, and had been in use since 1955. It was adopted as the emblem of the European Union in 1986. Belgium, France, Germany, Italy, Luxembourg and the Netherlands were the first to join the union in 1958, while more recent additions include: the Czech Republic, Cyprus, Estonia, Hungary, Latvia, Lithuania, Malta, Poland, Slovakia, and Slovenia.

Commonwealth of Nations

Ratio 1:2

The Commonwealth of Nations is a large group of independent nations, most of them former British colonies, which for political, economic, and social reasons have formed a worldwide organization recognizing the British monarch as its head. The current Commonwealth flag displays an emblem in gold on a blue field, showing a globe with five latitudinal and five longitudinal lines on it. Around this are a series of gold rays in a shape forming the letter "C." These rays do not literally represent the number of countries in the Commonwealth, but signify the range and variety of ways in which these countries now cooperate around the world. The original emblem was designed by the Gemini News Service in London in 1972, and updated in 1989. In 2000, the current design was approved.

African Union

Ratio 2:3

The African Union is a successor to the Organization of African Unity (OAU), and was launched in 2002. It exists to promote cooperation between African states and to encourage sustainable development to raise the living standards of African peoples. The new Union retained the original flag of the OAU until 2010, when the flag was redesigned. The present flag depicts the African continent against a white sun, set inside a circle of 54 gold stars to represent the member states. The green background is derived from the old OAU tricolor, and symbolizes hope, while the white signifies peace, unity and the continent's bright future.

Organization of American States

Ratio 2:3

The Organization of American States (OAS) exists to promote unity and respect between the countries of the Americas. It dates back to the 1820s, when revolutionary leader Simón Bolívar fought to create a continent "united in heart." In 1890, the Commercial Bureau of American Republics was formed, which later evolved into the OAS. In 1948, 21 nations signed the OAS Charter; today the organization has expanded to include nations of the Caribbean and Canada. The current OAS flag displays a white circle within which is an arc of colorful folded flags, representing the member countries, on a royal blue field.

Association of Southeast Asian Nations

Ratio 2:3

The flag of the Association of South-East Asian Nations (ASEAN) shows a red circle, edged in white, on a blue field. Within the circle is a stylized depiction of ten rice stalks, representing the ten countries that now form the association: the founder members, Indonesia, Malaysia, the Philippines, Singapore, and Thailand, which formed the organization in 1967; Brunei and Vietnam, which joined later; and the newest members, Cambodia, Laos, and Myanmar (which joined in 1997). According to an official statement, all the colors of the member nations' flags are included in the ASEAN flag. The blue stands for peace and stability, while the red signifies courage and dynamism. Yellow is for prosperity, and white for purity.

Arab League

Ratio 1:2

Established in 1945, the Arab League (more formally known as the League of Arab States) exists to further common interests between Arab-speaking peoples and to promote unity between Arab nations. To date, it has 22 members: Algeria, Bahrain, Comoros, Djibouti, Egypt, Iraq, Jordan, Kuwait, Lebanon, Libya, Mauritania, Morocco,Oman, Palestine, Qatar, Saudi Arabia, Somalia, Sudan,Syria, Tunisia, United Arab Emirates, and Yemen. The Arab League flag features a white wreath in the center, secured by a white ribbon at the base. Within the wreath is a gold chain comprised of 22 links, encircling a white crescent moon with the horns pointing upward. The ground of the flag is green, a traditional color of Islam, while gold denotes prosperity, and white stands for peace.

Red Cross

Ratio 1:1

The red cross is the internationally recognized symbol of the Red Cross Movement. It consists of a simple red Greek cross on a white field. The idea came from a Swiss humanitarian campaigner, Jean Henri Dunant, who had witnessed the horrors of war at the Battle of Solferino in 1859. The symbol was adopted in 1863, when a conference met in Geneva to discuss improvements for the medical care of soldiers in war. Today, under the terms of the Geneva Convention, the emblem is a humanitarian symbol to be placed on medical and other vehicles and buildings to protect them from military attack.

Red Crescent

Ratio 1:1

Although the red cross was devised as a neutral symbol, the fact that it is a Christian one caused objections from Muslim nations. Instead, these countries adopted the Islamic symbol of a plain red crescent on a white field. Later, Israel requested the adoption of a Star of David, since both the Christian and the Muslim faiths were now represented. The Red Cross movement rejected this idea, arguing that this would lead to too many partisan symbols. However, the movement is now considering a new symbol with no religious or political connotations, in keeping with its original aim of neutrality.

The Olympic Flag

Ratio 2:3

The design of the Olympic flag shows five interlocking rings of blue, yellow, black, green, and red, on a white field. One or more of these colors appear on each of the flags of all the countries that take part in the games. The rings themselves stand for the five continents that join together to form the Olympic movement: Africa, the Americas, Asia, Europe, and Oceania. The flag was designed by Pierre de Fredy, a French educator and sportsman who had the idea of reviving the Olympic games, which were first held in the year 776 B.C. and were an important part of the culture of ancient Greece. The design of the flag was adopted in 1913, but it was first flown at the Antwerp games in 1920.

Further Reading

J. Bradley, R. Powers, *Flags of Our Fathers*, Pimlico: 2000.

W. Crampton, *Flags (Usborne Spotter's Guides)*, Usborne: 2003.

D. Cannon, *Flags of the Union: An Illustrated History*, Pelican: 1994.

D. Cannon, *Flags of the Confederacy: An Illustrated History*, Pelican: 1997.

C4: Flags and Visual Signs, Royal Yachting Association, 2001.

Eyewitness Handbooks: Flags, Dorling Kindersley: 1999.

Alfred Znamierowski, *The World Encyclopedia of Flags: The Definitive Guide to International Flags, Standards, Banners, and Ensigns*, Lorenz: 1999.

Alfred Znamierowski, *Flags Through the Ages: A Guide to the World of Flags, Banners, Standards, and Ensigns*, Lorenz: 2002.

Wilson, T., *Flags At Sea*, UN Naval Institute: 2000.

Websites

http://flagspot.net/

http://www.cia.gov/cia/publications/the-world-factbook/

http://www.crwflags.com/fotw/flags/

http://www.wave.net/upg/immigration/flags.html

http://www.worldatlas.com/aatlas/world.htm

Acknowledgments

I would like to thank Sophie Collins, Jason Hook, and Rebecca Saraceno at Ivy Press; and my father, Lt Cmdr Philip Greig, for his help and advice.